THE FOUNTAINS
of
PLEASURE

AL-SAYED HAROUN IBN
HUSSEIN AL-MAKHZOUMI

THE FOUNTAINS

of

PLEASURE

TRANSLATED AND ANNOTATED
BY HATEM EL-KHALIDI

SPHERE BOOKS LIMITED

SPHERE BOOKS LTD

Published by the Penguin Group
27 Wrights Lane, London W8 5TZ, England
Viking Penguin Inc., 40 West 23rd Street, New York, New York 10010, USA
Penguin Books Australia Ltd, Ringwood, Victoria, Australia
Penguin Books Canada Ltd, 2801 John Street, Markham, Ontario, Canada L3R 1B4
Penguin Books (NZ) Ltd, 182–190 Wairau Road, Auckland 10, New Zealand

Penguin Books Ltd, Registered Offices: Harmondsworth, Middlesex, England

Originally published by Vantage Press 1970
Published by Quartet Books Limited 1987
Published by Sphere Books Limited 1989
1 3 5 7 9 10 8 6 4 2

Printed and bound in Great Britain by
Richard Clay Ltd, Bungay, Suffolk

CONTENTS

Some of the sayings attributed by the author to the Prophet Mohammad may not be those which are classified as authentic by the great majority of Moslem theologians and scholars.

THIS book is a direct translation of an old Arabic manuscript which I came across in the private family library of a very good and personal friend, in a town in the Arabian Peninsula, which shall remain unnamed, at least for the present. It had been my habit, whenever and wherever possible, to search in such libraries, for records and manuscripts that described the ancient and medieval mining activities which had flourished in the Peninsula since before the times of King Solomon.[1]

The owner of the manuscript is an elderly man, who is the most prominent member of an old and very distinguished family. He is a deeply devout Moslem who believes that, although the manuscript may have some historical value because of its age, it is, nevertheless, a very wicked and blasphemous work, which advocates freely and enthusiastically many sexual practices and attitudes that are strictly forbidden by Islam, and thus, understandably, he does not wish for his name to be associated with it in any way.[2] He will not allow it to be taken away from his library to be publicly or privately shown, for fear that it may be traced back to him, as the cover and all the pages contain certain identification marks which will make this possible. He confided that at times, he felt the strongest urge to destroy the manuscript, so that its "heretical" connection with his family may be erased for ever.

Perhaps, at a future date, the owner can be convinced that in reality, the manuscript is a scholarly work of the highest caliber, as I believe, and that it should be exhibited and studied in its original form and language. This is felt to be mandatory, because the present translation was done in very great haste, due to the lack of time, and it does not do much justice to the original and beautiful style.

The full title of the manuscript in Arabic, and which appears at the bottom of the title page of this book, may be translated as follows: "THE FOUNTAINS OF PLEASURE (SWEETNESS) IN THE ARTS OF THE PASSIONS (LUSTS)." A preview of the subject matter is most eloquently presented by the author in his preface.

The only date that is inscribed on the manuscript is found on its front page, above the table of contents, and which reads as follows: "COPIED FROM AN ANCIENT MANUSCRIPT IN THE YEAR 1152 HIJRIYAH BY M. . . . . . H. . . . . ." This date corresponds to about 1724 A.D., and the owner informed me that M. . . . . . H. . . . .[3] was one of the most illustrious of his direct ancestors.

No actual date however is found in the text itself, to indicate when the manuscript was originally written. But there is one important clue which may set the approximate date of authorship with some accuracy. The author mentions an episode which he says happened during the time when he was in the service of the "BROTHER OF THE GREAT SALADIN."

In Arab and Islamic history, there is but one GREAT SALADIN,[4] and he is the conqueror of Jerusalem from the Crusaders, and who lived from 1137 — 1193 A.D. Thus the date of authorship may be set during that period or a few years later.

Jeddah, Saudi Arabia

NOTES

1. The translator is a geologist who has been engaged in mineral and petroleum exploration in the Arabian Peninsula for the last thirteen years.
2. It was on this basis of strict anonymity, and after a most solemn oath on the Holy Qur'an by the translator, that the owner allowed him to translate the manuscript.

3. These are not the man's true initials.

4. The Ayubidd Dynasty of Saladin which was established by him, spread its rule into Arabia and the Yemen, where one of his brothers was his Regent. Perhaps this is the man referred to by the author. The full name of Saladin in Arabic is SALAH U'DEEN AL AYUBI. He was a Kurd by birth, who was born at Tekrit on the Tigris River. In 1169 A.D., he succeeded his uncle Shiroh whom he helped to conquer Egypt (1167-1168), thus suppressing the Fatemite Khalifate, and he extended his conquests over Syria, Mesopotamia, and Arabia. He crushed the Latin Kingdom of Jerusalem, capturing the King, Guy de Lusignan, and occupied Jerusalem in 1187 A.D. Saladin's rise prompted the Emperor Frederick I, Philip II of France, and Richard I of England to undertake the Third Crusade. Acre was besieged, and fell in 1191; but Richard's campaign left Saladin master of Jerusalem, and a truce of three years was signed between the Crusaders and Saladin in 1192 A.D. The Ayubidd Dynasty lasted some sixty years only.

AUTHOR'S PREFACE

IN THE NAME OF ALLAH[1] THE MERCIFUL THE COMPASSIONATE[2]

KNOW YE, all of good faith, that Man was created to be an instrument and an example of the glory of Allah. He was made of flesh and blood and bone to remind him of his weakness and fallibility and of the greatness and strength of our Maker.

Allah is beautiful and loves beauty. If it was not so, He would not have made us as we are, and He would not have created the world as beautiful as it is. The Most Merciful also gave us minds in order to praise Him and serve Him. We must praise Him in prayers and incantations, and we must serve Him through good service to our fellow men. We must also praise Him by joyously accepting and perfecting the gifts of the senses and their pleasures which He has bestowed on all of us.

Know ye, that the character of the flesh has been made by our Glorious Maker, not to be denied, but to be enjoyed to the fullest. It is hideous and blasphemous to deny and reject Allah's gifts of the pleasures of the flesh and the senses, and may He always be thanked for these pleasures, which are like the twinkling stars and planets that shine into and illuminate the darkness of the night of life.

Know ye all, that the supreme pleasures of the flesh and the senses are those that arise from the practice of copulation of man and woman (AL JIMA'A). Copulation is the ultimate act which was designed by our Maker for the propagation of Humanity. It is an act so intricate and meaningful in humans, in contrast to the animals. Allah had made it so pleasurable and attractive so as to make it imperative to be practiced constantly. Every nerve and organ and muscle that can be used should partake in copulation. It is only thus that Allah can be more wholly thanked and praised for his bounties. It is only thus that all the senses that Allah has given us can be put to the use that the Most Merciful has intended. It is only thus that the copulation of humans can differ from that of the animals. But alas, although this should be known, it is generally not, and the practice of copulation among most humans resembles in all its details that of the dog, the cattle, the fowl and all the other animals. With those humans it is a hurried, instinctive, rather ugly, wild and a very brief encounter. The man gets scant pleasure and the woman none at all. The results are tensions in the muscles and organs and joints. Thus men are turned into nervous and oppressive beasts and women are turned into shrews.

It is only after my passion has been completely spent that I take my pen to write this treatise in the hope of the service it may bring to the glory of Allah and to Humanity. I seek no personal reward or advancement, and now that I am no longer affected subjectively by the pleasures of the senses and the urges of the flesh, I can write with greater objectivity and clarity on such a subjective matter. This is why I have waited for so long, and I am now entering my eightieth year on this Earth.

I feel that I am fully qualified to write on such an important matter, I have been a practitioner of copulation for the last sixty-five years. I am moreover a physician of repute and great experience, and I have counselled and treated both men and women from Al Andalus[3] to Al Sind[4] and north to Samarkand[5] and all through Arabia, and in The Yemen,[6] my home, where I am now writing and waiting for my fate.

I would estimate that I have enjoyed copulation with many hundreds of women and I have examined and counselled many more. Thus, with the help of Allah, I shall undertake this step in putting all this vast experience in the form of a treatise to help both the uninitiated and those who sincerely wish to better themselves in the copulatory arts, and may Allah in His infinite wisdom and graciousness bless us with His extra bounties, so that we may better praise Him and worship Him and enjoy His gifts.

Our great Prophet Mohammad, may he always be blessed, has shown us by his own words and deeds how Allah has meant us to enjoy copulation. The Prophet married several women and he enjoyed in copulation a countless number of slaves. He said: "HE WHO IS ABLE TO ENJOY COPULATION, AND DOES NOT DO SO FOR ANY REASON, IS NOT OF ME AND HE HAS LOST HIS EARTHLY PARADISE."

Our gracious Prophet also said: "BLESSED IS THE PASSIONATE, RESPONSIVE WOMAN IN COPULATION AND BLESSED IS THE MAN WHO TAUGHT HER AND THEY BOTH SHALL GLORY IN ALLAH'S GIFTS."

I have read most of the literature that has been published on copulation and I have found that most of the authors are either extremely vulgar or sadly uninformed in these matters.[8] This has prompted me more than ever towards what I consider a noble endeavour, and may Allah grant me the time and the energy to finish it before I pass away.

This treatise shall have two purposes. The first and foremost is to describe in detail the true nature and practice of the art of human copulation, which will result in making the act of supreme pleasure to both the man and the woman. It must be emphasized that it is the man's duty to instruct the woman in these arts, for without his instruction the woman, with her simple mind and lack of imagination, will not be capable of bringing these pleasures to herself and to the man. However, the best instruction that the man can give is by acting expertly himself and the woman will learn by imitating him. Otherwise, the man will have to be content with a woman who in copulation may act like a placid cow.

The second purpose is to bring to the reader a glimpse of the science of procreation and the realities of human reproduction, with another glimpse of the various and common morbid conditions of the human reproductive organs and their possible avoidance and cure. I shall also describe very briefly the many aberrations that afflict some men and women.

My time on this earth is running short and I shall curb the tendency towards garrulousness which is normal when writing on such matters. This treatise may be found to be too short by many. However, I shall attempt to include all the knowledge on matters related to the man and the woman in quest of each other, that I have been able to gather during my long and busy life.

As I begin now, I again ask Allah the Almighty for His help and blessing and, above all, for His mercy.

NOTES

1. The Supreme Being (God) of the Moslems.
2. This is the opening sentence of the Holy Qur'an, and of every one of its chapters, and it is the opening sentence of all the writings of devout Moslem authors.
3. Al Andalus is the Arabic name for Spain.
4. The northwest part of the Indian Sub-Continent, in which the Indus River flows.
5. A city in West Asia, now in the Uzbek Republic of the Soviet Union. The city became a great center of Arab and Islamic civilization until it was destroyed by Genghis Khan in the 13th century A.D., and in 1370 A.D. Tamarlane made it his capital. It was during his reign that Samarkand reached its zenith.
6. A country in the southwestern part of the Arabian Peninsular. It is fertile and mountainous and was called Arabia Felix by the Romans.
7. The word used here by the Prophet Mohammad was AL NIKAH which means legal copulation with wives or slaves. Islam strictly forbids copulation outside of marriage and prescribes severe punishment for the adulterer and adulteress. Copulation with slaves was permitted, but never against their will, and once the slave became pregnant, her master had to marry her in order to legitimize the

child. Islam allows polygamy with a maximum of four wives, in accordance with the words of the Holy Qur'an: "MARRY OF THE WOMEN WHO SEEM ATTRACTIVE TO YOU TWO OR THREE OR FOUR; AND IF YOU FEAR THAT YOU MAY NOT DO JUSTICE, THEN ONLY ONE, OR WHAT YOUR RIGHT HAND POSSESSES (SLAVES OR CAPTIVES). THUS IT IS MORE LIKELY THAT YOU WILL NOT DO INJUSTICE."

8. This is true, for although Arabic literature is full of various works of light sexual entertainment and pornography, both in poem and prose, there are no known works with the approach to the study of sex in humans, as this one.

THE FOUNTAINS
of
PLEASURE

CHAPTER 1

OF THE STRUCTURE OF WOMEN AND MEN*

"Beautiful for mankind is love of the passions that come from women and love of offspring, and stored heaps of gold and silver, and branded horses and cattle and land. That is comfort of the life of the world. And with Allah is a more excellent abode."

THE HOLY QUR'AN

THE WOMAN

THE HUMAN RACE was created by Allah the Almighty and is composed almost equally of men and women; males and females. Allah has endowed them with specialised organs of copulation and procreation which are a marvel and a miracle in structure and function, and this attests further to the glory of Our Creator.

* * *

Man is a thinking and feeling being and, in copulation, he must bring in his thoughts and feelings as well as his organs. It is only the animals which copulate instinctively and without thought or feelings.

* * *

Islam, the only true Religion, has recognized that copulation must always be a pleasurable activity, which must not be denied to any man or woman. No person need deny himself or herself voluntarily[1] of such pleasures in the false belief that by doing thus, he or she can get nearer to Allah, to

23

serve Him and glorify Him better by such cruel denial. In Islam there are no such abominable practices. Our Prophet, may his name be blessed has said: "MAN GETS A GLIMPSE OF HEAVEN WHEN HE IS IN THE ARMS OF A SOFT, BEAUTIFUL AND PASSIONATE WOMAN "

*　　*　　*

The woman, like the man, is endowed with her own organs of copulation and procreation. She is meant fully to enjoy[2] and not only bear copulation for the sake of procreation as some false apostles have preached. Allah has blessed the passionate responsive woman, and in copulation she must feel and give pleasure equally. She can do that however, only if she is instructed freely and joyously by the man. Instinct alone will not serve her well. And a woman's beauty should bring delight to herself and her lover.

*　　*　　*

Allah has endowed women with thin and sensitive skins. Thus their feelings when kissed, stroked, fondled, caressed, bitten or licked are much more pleasurable than in man. The woman's hairless body with its soft and flowing curves, offers unlimited delights to her and to the eyes, hands, tongue and the penis of the man. Praise be to Allah and our thanks to Him for all these gifts.

*　　*　　*

The woman was created by Allah from Adam's rib so that she would be his helpmate in his abode, to produce his children and to be his pleasure and delight in his bed. If the woman is happy and satisfied in copulation, she will be happy in all her other activities. She will gladly bear children and her births will be easy[3]. She will be content to wait for her husband or lover or master to embrace her and daily she will thank Allah for her lot. She will be a good wife, a good companion, a good mother and a good Human. She will be serene and kind and soft, and at peace with the world and with herself.

*　　*　　*

Now I shall describe in brief the organs of copulation and procreation of the woman, and the function of each. First I shall describe the external parts and continue inwards:

The vulva (AL FARJ) is the external part of the woman's organs, and it is located between her anus and pubic bone.

The vulva is composed of an outer pair of vertical lips[4] (AL SHAFFAH AL KHARIJIYYAH), and an inner pair of lips[5] (AL SHAFFAH AL DAKILIYYAH). At the outer junction of the inner lips lies a small but extremely sensitive and important organ, the clitoris (AL BADHR).

There are two orifices in the body of the vulva and these are concealed by the inner and outer lips. The one above is very small and it is the opening of the urinary canal. The other, which is lower and about two fingers width up from the anus, is the orifice of the vagina (BAB AL MAHBAL). This orifice in the virgin is partially covered with a membrane which is called the hymen (GHASHA' ALBAKARAH), and which varies in character from woman to woman. All these organs and structures are made of extremely thin and sensitive skin which gives voluptuous feelings when gently stroked, fondled, licked and kissed, but which will be tender and painful to the touch if roughly handled.

The vagina (AL MAHBAL) is a flexible canal which can extend inwards to receive the full length of the man's erect penis, but only if it is relaxed and moist. The maximum flexed size varies greatly from one woman to another.

At the end of the vagina is the orifice of the uterus (BAB AL RAHM), which is the entrance to the uterus (AL RAHM), and where the child is carried in pregnancy. The uterus is connected to the two ovaries (AL MABAYED) which are situated on each side of the uterus and in front of the kidneys. I will not go any further in anatomical descriptions since it is of no direct interest to us in this treatise. I will only add that such intricate and complex structures, which still harbour many mysteries,[6] should always make us think with intense humbleness and constant remembrance of the greatness and infinite wisdom of the Almighty Allah.

Another structure which must be mentioned and which is related to procreation, and is indeed a very pleasant accessory in copulation, is the breast of the woman.

The perfectly formed ones are a delight to hold, kiss, fondle and such at. But alas! these structures quickly lose their shapes and become ugly and pendulous with the advance of age.

*　　*　　*

The only real function of the breast is to produce milk for the nourishment of the infant. In this capacity they serve most of the time with great adequacy, if the woman is happy and contented. The milk will turn sour if the woman is nervous, sickly or a shrew. Our Prophet has said: "BLESSED IS THE WOMAN WITH SWEET FLOWING MILK, FOR SHE IS FEEDING HER INFANT THE NECTAR OF ALLAH. AND MAY ALLAH CURSE THE SHREW WHOSE MILK HAS THE TASTE OF HELL'S BRIMSTONE."

*　　*　　*

Women's breasts come in a great variety of shapes and sizes. I do not know why Allah in His wisdom has ordained thus, since all breasts serve but one purpose, and that is to produce milk for the infant. However, I can say and I believe, that the shape and the size of the breast of any woman is predestined from her birth. It may be that she inherits this shape and size from one ancestor or that the shape and size is a composite of the shapes and sizes of all her ancestors. Only Allah knows for sure.

*　　*　　*

A common type of breast is the rounded one which resembles a mature pomegranate.[7] In virgins this breast is beautiful to behold and to hold and the nipple and aureole are not blemished by use. The breasts are separated by a de-

26

lightful valley which gives rise to the rounded swells on both sides. In profile this breast is a picture of the symmetry of roundness and the lower part is not resting on the wall of the chest, but swings freely above it. This breast has the least tendency to become pendulous with the suckling of infants and the encroachment of middle age.

*　　　*　　　*

Another type of breast which is not common is the half moon, which, when looked at either from the front or the side, resembles a half moon. It is curved upwards and has the tendency to pendulousness with continued use and advancement in age.

*　　　*　　　*

The third type of breast is that which looks in profile like a fig; small and pointed. This breast will increase in size when the woman starts to produce milk after her delivery. However, after the cessation of the milk it shrinks back and becomes wrinkled like a dry plum.

*　　　*　　　*

The breast that resembles that of a goat is seen on some women. It always has very long and dark nipples. The breast is long and narrow and pendulous, even in virgins, and it will rest on the woman's chest, pointing downwards, and it will reach the woman's thighs when she sits down. Alas! I have never liked the sight of such a breast, for it looks more animal than human.

*　　　*　　　*

Some women are endowed with enormous breasts resembling watermelons. The valley between these breasts will be a very narrow gorge. Women who possess such breasts may be thin or stout and they are prone to various afflictions of the chest and to growths and ulcers in their breasts and this usually occurs in one breast or the other, but very rarely in both.

*　　　*　　　*

Lastly, there are women who possess no breasts at all and their chests resemble those of immature and hairless boys. However, they may be endowed with large nipples and some of these women in late pregnancy will develop breasts which may not grow very big, but which will produce abundant milk. Once these women stop suckling, their breasts will shrink back to nothingness and what remains on their chests will be two long and drooping nipples.

* * *

The nipples of women's breasts come in various sizes and shades of color, and shapes. There is also variation in the size and color of the aureoles.

Some nipples thicken outwardly, while others are pointed, and some women have nipples that are buried into their breasts and this will make it impossible for these women to suckle their infants. Such women are, however, very few in number.

* * *

There are aureoles which cover a very small round area around the nipples, while others may cover almost half the area of the breasts themselves.

* * *

The color of the nipples and aureoles of virgin breasts is usually that of a pale red rose. However, some time after defloration the color will change to a very light shade of reddish brown. This is perhaps due to the absorption in some way by the woman of the fluids of the man, which causes the color change.[8]

* * *

Some women have hairs growing on the sides of their nipples and on the aureoles and these hairs at times reach the length of half a finger. When these hairs are plucked they will grow back very slowly.

* * *

28

Now I shall describe briefly the different forms and shapes that normal women come in:

There are first the women who are well hipped and thin waisted. Such women usually will have small and narrow chests with thin delicate and elegant shoulders, and long and well moulded necks. They are beauties to behold and great delights to their lovers. Their legs are straight and of proportionate shape, tapering downwards to fine, thin ankles like those of gazelles.[9] Such women are usually of good or noble birth and they could be short or tall in stature.

*　　*　　*

Secondly there are the wide hipped, thick waisted and big chested women, who usually possess thick legs and ankles. Such women are very sturdy and will have easy births, unless their infants come in breached positions. They will more than likely be of peasant or other humble stock.

*　　*　　*

There are the women who are very narrow hipped, like boys, and with thick waists and small chests, and with short or long legs which are very slender. Because they are small and thin their vulvas may appear to be enormous. These women are destined to have very difficult births due to the narrowness of their birth canals.[10] Allah help them and may He ease their pains and sufferings, and may He enfold them in His mercy.

*　　*　　*

Bow legs can occur in any type of woman, also among men. The bending of the bones occurs in infanthood due to unknown[11] and mysterious causes and nothing can be done to straighten the limbs once they are bent.

*　　*　　*

There are some women who possess very hairy bodies like men, and especially on their limbs. Some have hair on their chests and between their breasts and on the nipples and aureoles. Some women have soft fur-like hair which covers large parts of their shoulders and backs.

Other women have hair on their upper lips and faces and are able to grow beards like men. However, their vulvas may be completely formed in every detail. Thus it cannot be said that the growth of hair on women is because these women lack in femininity.

* * *

Let it be known that there are creatures who are not full men or full women, but a combination of both. These are the hermaphrodites (AL AKNATH), whom I shall describe later. Let us thank Allah that these are few in number, whose lives are an agony to themselves and to their families.

* * *

Our great Prophet has said: "BLESSED IS THE HAIRY MAN AND THE SMOOTH HAIRLESS WOMAN WHO IS A DELIGHT OF SIGHT AND TOUCH."

* * *

There are various types of vulvas in women. In structure, however, there are three distinct types that can be differentiated and classified.

* * *

The domed vulva (DHAT AL QUBBAH) is the one that is situated high up and starts directly below the pubic bone. It is very prominent and domed. Looking at it directly from the front and with the woman's legs together, the upper junction of the outer lips can be plainly seen. This vulva is proud looking and deliciously so, and when the woman's thighs are spread apart it looks even more protruding and proud.

* * *

The heavy lipped vulva (DHAT AL SHAFAH) is the one that has very large and fat outer lips. It is sometimes seen on very small women and the contrast in sizes is quite breathtaking and pleasantly so.[12]

30

However, the size of the vulva has actually nothing to do with the size of the vaginal orifice, which could be very small and tight, while the vulval lips could be very big.

*　　*　　*

The slipped or receded vulva (AL MOUNZALIQAH), is the one that is situated rather low. The upper part, which is the junction of the outer lips, is invisible when the woman is standing with her thighs together. This vulva is only revealed when the woman spreads her thighs apart. Thus it can be seen to start well below the pubic bone.

This vulva is usually small with delicate looking lips, but the vaginal orifice may be quite wide and accommodating.

*　　*　　*

The various types of vulvas can be crossed to form an infinite variety of shapes to include the character of any number of the three basic types. What can be said is that no two women's vulvas are alike.

I must say, subjectively, that however and whatever their structure, vulvas are the sweetest organs in this world.

*　　*　　*

In most of the erotic literature of the vulgar and the ignorant numerous classifications and descriptions and names for vulvas are mentioned. These assigned names, usually coincide with the actions that these vulvas are reported to perform on the man's penis during copulation, such as biting, sucking, kneading and squeezing, as if these vulvas were free and independent structures, capable of voluntary action of their own free will.

This is pure nonsense, as I shall show later, and these names and descriptions are either given in jest or to arouse the excitation of the reader.

Other writers have classified vulvas more elaborately and poetically by giving them names of various beautiful birds and animals.[13] Such purpose is also to arouse the reader's passion rather than to instruct him and add to his knowledge.

*　　*　　*

31

The color of the outer lips of the vulva varies with different women. The color may be dark brown to cherry red, this latter being the most pleasant of all colors, in my opinion. These colors will change in their shades with the degree of excitation of the woman,[14] and what was originally brown may become reddish brown, and what was cherry red: that vulva will become fiery red and such is the most exciting and enticing color that is made to add to a man's fire.

*   *   *

On peeling or parting the outer lips of the vulva, the inner lips are revealed and these will possess the color of a red rose, and as a color the shades will differ from vulva to vulva, as it does from rose to rose. The color of the virgin's inner lips is usually very pale, like that of a red rose in early bloom. This shade becomes darker when the virginity is lost and with the frequent trips of the penis into the vagina.

*   *   *

The inner lips will change color temporarily when excitation occurs, and the lips will swell and open and the color will become more intense and vivid as passion builds up in the woman.

What a beautiful sight is this lovely creation of Allah, the vulva, and what pleasures it promises in its swelling and opening and moistening.

*   *   *

The hymen (GHASHA' AL BAKARAH) is the principal gate to all sexual pleasures. It is a cover and a protector to the vagina and it is found in the overwhelming majority of virgins. There are, however, those very fortunate few who are born without it and thus they will not bleed during their first time of copulation. This will give rise to the suspicion of the husbands or masters, that such women were not virgins when they married or purchased them and the consequences may be grave for all.[15] May Allah in His mercy ease the burdens of such women and grant them understanding and

32

compassion from all concerned. Such women will usually feel no pain when they are first entered and perhaps pleasure may be felt if they have knowledgeable partners.

* * *

Hymens are of four basic types as regards their structure. In all these types the character of the membrane varies from very thin to quite thick, which will make defloration (FADHAL BAKARAH) very difficult and painful and sometimes impossible because the pain may become too much for the woman to bear. In this case she will surely thrash about in great agony if the man will persist. Fortunately such cases are very rare. It has been said and wisely: "TO DEFLOWER DOES NOT MEAN TO INJURE AND MAIM. THE ACT SHOULD BE ONE OF TENDERNESS AND UNDERSTANDING AND PERHAPS PLEASURE."

Another very ancient saying goes as follows: "TO ENSURE EVERLASTING LOVE AND DEVOTION FROM THE WOMEN, DEFLOWER HER WITH THE UTMOST OF TENDERNESS, FOR LOVE DIES ON THE FIRST NIGHT IF PAIN SHALL REPLACE PLEASURE."

The first type of hymen can be seen to resemble the new moon. It is the one that lies covering the mouth of the vagina, and it has one long curved slit in it, which resembles the curve of the new moon.

* * *

The second type of hymen is the one that covers the mouth of the vagina and it possesses not more than two or three irregularly shaped perforations which have ragged edges and perhaps a small finger can easily be passed through these slits.

* * *

There is the hymen which covers the whole opening of the vagina. It is perforated with many small holes, perhaps up to fifteen, thus resembling a sieve.

* * *

Finally, there is the hymen that covers only part of the opening of the vagina. In some women it is merely a flap or loose skin. Defloration of this type is the easiest, as there is no real barrier to the penis and there may be no bleeding, or perhaps very little, when the penis is first introduced into the vagina.

*　　*　　*

Very rarely, a girl is born with the hymen completely blocking and sealing the vaginal canal. The first time that this condition will be noticed is when the girl reaches puberty (AL IBLAGH) and starts her menstrual cycle (AL HAYDH). Blood will initially accumulate in the vagina and then will back up into the uterus. Great discomfort and bloating and sometimes much pain is felt. If this condition is not treated promptly, by cutting open the hymen to let the blood drain out, the girl will surely die when the blood finally retreats up into her body and putrefies and will poison her system. Fortunately these cases are very easy to cure, thanks to Allah.

*　　*　　*

The clitoris is the seat and the first key to the woman's voluptuous feelings. It is strange and exciting to realise that such a small appendage is greatly responsible for the initiation of the woman's pleasure in copulation.

All other organs are secondary, with the exception of the vagina, which will produce in the woman feelings of utter voluptuousness if it is stimulated for a long time by the man's penis.

The clitoris is a vital organ of pleasure and may Allah curse those barbarians in Egypt and other countries[16] who cut off the clitoris of their girls before they reach maturity and thus deprive them of their rights for the feelings of pleasure in copulation, these feelings which are the gift of Allah to all women. Thus these gelded women are transformed into unfeeling and resentful creatures and copulation with

34

them is like uniting with a corpse. Such are horrors almost too much to conceive.

*   *   *

The clitoris is located at the upper junction of the inner lips of the vulva.

The clitoris, in shape and action, can be said in a general way to resemble the penis of the man.[17] It becomes hard and swells and stands erect like the penis when it is fondled or when the woman becomes aroused in passion. It has a small head which resembles that of the penis, although there is no orifice in it; the organ is completely blind.

*   *   *

The average length of the clitoris is something like the width of two small fingers and with a diameter or thickness of a small boy's finger. These dimensions are when it is in a state of erection.

Most of the clitoris is embedded into the flesh of the woman's vulva and only its head sticks out from between the junction of the lips. In some women the foreskin which covers the head, like the foreskin of an uncircumcised penis, completely covers and hides the head and then it is not evident to the eyes, and in erection it is felt as a raised small lump between the lips of the vulva.

There are cases, which are not very rare, where the clitoris is of very large proportions and it may look like the penis of a young boy. When such a clitoris is in a state of erection it is of a magnificent size and the woman who possesses such a clitoris is usually filled with burning passion, and she is insatiable in copulation.[18]

Every man should possess such a woman, but only for a short time, as her performance in copulation is a revelation of lustful movements and heavings to thrill any man's heart. However, this woman will ultimately wear out even the strongest man with her unlimited desires and she will surely

35

seek others under the compulsion of her turbulent needs. May Allah grant that this should never happen to a true believer.

Such women must ultimately be pitied as they cannot control their lustful drives and either they will be killed by their husbands or masters, or they will go mad with passion and kill themselves,[19] and may Allah forgive them.

I shall now describe the vulva and how it changes in character with the arousal of passion and in copulation, and what feelings it gives to the woman by its manipulation and use by the man.

*   *   *

The clitoris is the seat of the initial voluptuous feelings that engulf the woman who is being caressed or copulated with. The clitoris, when thus aroused or only by lascivious thoughts going on in the mind of the woman, will swell and stiffen and become very sensitive to the touch. I have asked women to describe their actual feelings when their clitorises are being manipulated and they answered that these feelings were akin to waves of swelling pleasure, which start at the tip of the clitoris and then invade into the rest of their bodies. These waves go deep via the vagina and up the uterus and into the anus, spreading to the buttocks and then move downwards to their thighs. Some women will feel these waves go down to their toes which will then curl involuntarily.

Waves of pleasure will also permeate upwards to the trunk of the body and to the breasts and to the aureoles and nipples, which will swell and become erect. Fondling the nipples may then produce a most delightful counter-wave which will swell downwards towards the clitoris. These two waves will meet in the core of the uterus, which together with the vagina will pulsate and there is where the most intense pleasures develop and which will lead to the orgasm (AL SHABAQ).[20] This is the most intense type of orgasm, as I shall describe later.

Pleasures as the result of the manipulation of the clitoris may go upwards to the neck and face of the woman and her hair roots will become sensitive. The woman's lips will swell slightly and assume a greater sensitivity and her nostrils will

36

flare like those of a mare in heat. Her lips, when kissed and licked and sucked by the man, will give her much pleasurable feelings. Some women will also feel pleasure seeping into their arms and to the palms of their hands and up to their finger tips.

The outer lips of the vulva will swell and open and change in color and the inner lips will be revealed and they will also swell and soften and open up, revealing the vaginal orifice. This will be like the blooming of a beautiful flower. Ah! what a wonderful sight it is and how perfect is Allah's creation.

*　　*　　*

All the time, since the initiation of the man's actions or because of the woman's yearnings and thoughts alone, lubricating fluids will pour out from various places in the vulva and principally from the orifice of the vagina.[21] These fluids, in all women if they are young and healthy and clean, are of a very distinct and pleasant and exciting smell and of a slightly salty taste, which once savoured will never be forgotten. The fluids are sticky and milky white in colour, and may be slightly viscous or as mucus.

Obviously the purpose of these fluids is to lubricate and thus facilitate the entry of the penis and to make its journey into the vagina pleasurable for both the man and the woman.

What delights await such a man and woman, from the moment of the blossoming of the vulva. It will truly be a trip into the garden of delights and Allah will always bless such a journey.

*　　*　　*

The outer lips of the vulva are relatively insensitive when compared with the clitoris and although they will swell as a reaction to manipulation, such manipulation produces only moderate feelings of delight, but the woman will become aware of the man's touch and intentions and this will excite her greatly.

*　　*　　*

37

The inner lips are sensitive and their inner folds, which are rooted to the woman's body, will produce feelings of great pleasure when manipulated by the man.

* * *

The orifice of the urethra in most women is sensitive. However, pleasure is felt only if the lubrication of the vulva is complete, and the area is stroked and rubbed very gently. Only irritation will result if dry fingers are used to caress this orifice.

* * *

The vaginal orifice is very sensitive and such sensitivity is located not only in the opening, but all through the vaginal canal, when the woman is aroused. The orifice then becomes flaccid and ready to receive the erect penis. A very warm and intense feeling of voluptuousness will be felt by the woman as the man's penis pushes deeper into the canal and the moist skin of the canal will stretch to accommodate the penis in its full thrust forward. If the penis is long enough and the coital position is favourable, the penis will reach the mouth of the uterus where it must stop.

* * *

The man must insure that he has very short finger nails before he attempts to caress the vulva, as long nails will cut and abrade this very soft tissue and irritation rather than pleasure will be the result.

* * *

Allah has created the vulva to be caressed and manipulated by the man. It is permissible for him and more exciting in many ways, as it is for the woman, if he uses his lips, teeth and tongue in caressing the vulva.[22]

There are those uninspired and dull people who advocate that such practice is immodest, immoral and abnormal. I do not agree at all, and I think it is normal and moral and is to be encouraged, because it is such a delightful experience for both the man and the woman.

The vulva is an organ of supreme delights and if it is healthy it is as clean as the mouth of the man and the woman. I see no reason for preventing the mouth and vulva from meeting in a joyous caress. The vulva is the entrance to the sacred organs of procreation and these organs are not dirty or loathsome, so why should the vulva be considered untouchable to the lips of man?

On the contrary, the vulva must be revered by man, because it is from whence he came out into the world. It is the entrance of the organs that Allah has bestowed on woman for the perpetuation of the Human Race to Eternity.

What fools are those who say that the vulva should not be touched and caressed by the lips of the man.

Those unfortunates who miss this blessed caress of the man to the woman miss touching and smelling and tasting the sweetest nectar. They miss bestowing a gesture so exquisite and fine, which is the most loving gesture that a man can bestow on his beloved woman before entering her and fulfilling her.

* * *

The man does not touch and caress the woman's vulva as soon as they meet. Only brutes will attempt that. The man, rather, must first prepare her as I shall show later. But when the time comes and he will know when she is ready, and she will welcome it and her vulva will become moist and will swell and blossom.

* * *

Care must be taken not to start caressing the vulva when it is dry. Being thus should be a warning to the man that the woman is unready and perhaps unresponsive to his advances. Thus, if the man will persist, only a feeling of irritation will result.

The caressing of the clitoris when the area is dry will also result only in irritating the woman.

However, when the vulva is felt to be moist, start your fingers on caressing it as a whole. Get hold of all of it with

39

your hand and squeeze it gently. Let your fingers linger into the inner folds of the lips and gently but firmly stroke these areas.

Return now to the clitoris and apply pressure to it, moving your fingers to and fro on it. Take the clitoris between your thumb and forefinger and squeeze it gently. It should now be completely erect and pulsating.

Roll the clitoris between the thumb and forefinger, caressing the vulva as a whole simultaneously. The woman will now be feeling extreme excitation and will abandon herself to your embrace.[23] Keep up this motion, slowly at first, then faster, but still gently and firmly. At the same time keep running your fingers up and down the vulva lips, both on their inside and outside. Get your fingers into occasional forays into the vaginal orifice.

And remember that these caresses should be done without rough or hard or abrupt movement and pressures. Otherwise the magic will be lost and irritation will set in.

*   *   *

Now the time has come to bestow that sweet caress of your mouth to the vulva and this should be done with extreme delicacy of movements and gestures.

Bring your mouth down and flick your tongue along the lips of the vulva on the outside and inside, which you will expose with your finger tips.

Give the vulval lips, which must now be swollen and ready, the loving bites with your teeth and suck at them with your lips.

SAVOUR THE AROMA AND THE TASTE OF THIS MAGNIFICENT AND BEAUTIFUL ORGAN.

Bring your mouth to the clitoris and catch it in your teeth. Gently pull on it, then let your tongue encircle it.

Hold the clitoris between your lips and suck at it, taking it deep into your mouth and then rhythmically suck it in and out of your mouth.

Keep your fingers busy in caressing the lips and the flesh of the vulva with more frequent forays into the vaginal orifice.

*   *   *

The vaginal orifice is best stimulated by initially inserting one finger and slowly rotating it around the orifice. When the orifice relaxes, two fingers or perhaps three can be bunched up and inserted and rolled around its walls. This movement should be increased in speed, but not too fast and never in a harsh and abrupt manner.

*   *   *

Continue to keep the mouth busy with the clitoris and suck at it rhythmically and keep caressing the rest of the vulva. This will produce no end to the delight and excitation of the woman and she may soon reach her first orgasm.

*   *   *

Besides the vulva, the breasts of the woman, when manipulated expertly, will produce feelings of intense pleasure, second only to the feelings produced by the manipulation of the clitoris.[24] Allah has thus ordained, so that the women may derive intense pleasure which shall keep them interested in feeding their infants. The drive towards pleasure through nursing is so strong that the women cannot be swayed to neglect their children. Allah be praised for putting a purpose in all his creations and designs.

*   *   *

The feelings of pleasure in the breast of the women are mainly concentrated in the nipples and aureoles. These are the structures which the infant takes into his mouth to suck at.

Most women report that this action of the infant at their breast produces in them intense feelings of voluptuousness which permeates into their whole bodies and chiefly into the uterus and the vagina and as far as down as the tip of the clitoris. Most women will feel their uterus pleasurably contracting while nursing, or while a man is sucking at their breasts.

There is no more beautiful or rapturous look than on the face of the woman who is nursing the infant. At times this look may become quite lustful and the eyes of the woman may be seen to cloud with passion and one may see tremors of delight go through her body while engaged thus.

I have been told by many women that they feel orgasms occasionally while nursing their infants. A few women experience orgasms every time they suckle their children.

*　　*　　*

The breasts should be freed from any binding that surrounds them or hides them and they should swing freely when you are ready to caress them. Only thus can full enjoyment be obtained for you and the woman.

Hold the breast with your hand and squeeze it gently and then knead it. Roll the nipple between your thumb and forefinger until it becomes swollen and erect. Gently rub at the base of the breast where it joins the wall of the chest. Kiss and lick at the valley between the breasts. These areas are also sensitive and they become more so when the nipples are erect.

Now blow your breath over the nipple and then take it into your mouth. Pass your tongue over the nipple and aureole and wet them thoroughly with your saliva. The woman will have the most voluptuous feelings when all these parts are very wet.

Suck, first slowly, at the nipple and then more vigorously and enclose your lips and mouth over the whole of the aureole and draw the breast deep into your mouth. At the same time knead at the breast with your fingers as an infant does to his mother.

Keep up the suction at the nipple and aureole vigorously, but be gentle enough to avoid pain or irritation to the breast. Do not let your teeth inadvertently take a deep bite at the nipple, although taking delicate nips once in a while will increase the woman's delights. And always keep the whole area very moist with your saliva.

You can judge the degree of excitation of the woman by the way she behaves now. If she places a hand on the back of your head and neck and draws your mouth closer to her breast, she is experiencing great pleasure. She will now be heaving deep sighs and she may start to writhe instinctively.

* * *

In the exchange of caresses between the man and the woman there is nothing sweeter than kissing each other on the lips and in the mouth.[25]

The lips and mouths of men and women are very sensitive to the touch of each other and much pleasure and excitation will be reaped if this is done with finesse and expertise.

Women appear to have more sensitive mouths than men and they derive much more pleasure from kissing. This may explain why women like to linger in their kissing with no apparent desire, until much later, for copulation, while the man tries quickly and will feel an urgent desire to copulate after very little preliminary kissing. Kissing does not actually satisfy him, but will goad him onwards towards more urgent desires.

Virgins, especially, derive all the satisfaction that they yearn for from kissing, if no other part of their body is stimulated. However, an experienced woman will want and desire copulation urgently after she is satisfied with kissing.

The kiss (AL QBLAH) starts as the touch of the man's lips to the woman's lips and their noses should fit snugly against each other, and thus the lips will lay on each other along their entire length.

Movements of the man's lips on the woman's lips may now be initiated and a small amount of saliva may be pushed out by his tongue to make the contact between the lips wet. This will make the lips more sensitive and the contact will be more pleasurable.

The experienced woman will now open her mouth and in

so doing she will discharge the saliva that had been accumulating in her mouth, into the man's mouth.

Both tongues will now lash at each other and caress each other and there is a continuous exchange of sweet saliva between the two mouths.

*　　*　　*

I must stress here that it is absolutely essential for the mouths of the man and the woman to be very fresh and clean before attempting any form of kissing. If a meal has been partaken of which contained foods that leaves pungent odors and tastes in the mouth, such as onions, garlic and spices, then extra care should be taken to wash away these odors and tastes. All food particles should be removed from between the teeth and the mouth should be washed on the inside and outside with soap and water, and then it should be rinsed many times with rose water.

*　　*　　*

There is nothing sweeter and tastier and more thrilling than to savour the loved one's saliva, but if the mouth is dirty and the loved one's saliva is foul, there is nothing more unpleasant than to kiss such a mouth. Alas! many people forget this and they will hasten to do their kissing soon after they have finished their meal.

The prophet has said: "DIRTY MOUTHS AND BODIES OF MEN AND WOMEN ARE THE SCOURGE OF THEIR LOVE." How true!

Allah has said: "CLEANNESS IS AKIN TO FAITH." So take heed all Ye of good faith.[26]

*　　*　　*

As you proceed in kissing, open your mouth wide and suck the woman's lips into it. Have your tongue travel all over her mouth and into the areas between her lips and teeth, as these are very sensitive areas. Let the woman do the same to you and savour her tongue and its caresses. You must not be impatient and hurried in your kissing, as nothing

44

puts a woman more in readiness for copulation than this sweet caress.

* * *

In kissing, you and the woman will pay each other homage by mingling your mouths and breaths together. You will be breathing almost as one person and this should intensify your desires and pleasures and you will be brought forward to the crest of your journey into ecstasy.

* * *

The area between the orifice of the vagina and the anus is quite sensitive and will produce pleasurable feelings if stroked, especially during copulation. This should be accompanied by trips with your finger into the vagina while the penis is in. The tightening of the orifice thus, may bring the penis to bear more pressure on the clitoris.

This caress is especially beneficial if the penis is thin or the vaginal orifice too large. It is also of benefit if the position of the man in relation to the woman is such that the penis is not exerting enough pressure on the clitoris.

* * *

The anus of the woman is made of very delicate and sensitive skin which is similar to that of the vulva and the lips of the mouth. This orifice in women, when stroked gently, may produce spasms of pleasure that will be felt in the vagina. It should be remembered that this area must be thoroughly cleaned before copulation.

* * *

Downwards from the vulva, the thighs of the woman are sensitive and this is mostly along their inside. These limbs are round and soft in women and very seductive looking and they are a great delight to behold and caress. They should be touched, fondled, kissed, bitten and licked and this can be done during the caressing of the vulva with the hands and mouth before copulation. During the vulval caress with the mouth, the hands and fingers should be run back and forth

45

along them and this should give the woman greatly added excitement.

During copulation and when in a position to do so, the thighs may be pinched, stroked and kissed.

* * *

Further down from the thighs, there stretch the knees and calves and feet. The calves, when shapely, are very exciting to the man, as is every part of a beautiful woman's body. The feet may be stroked and tickled and this will add to the enjoyment and abandon.

* * *

Up from the vulva, the hips swell inwards into the tiny waist of the woman and this may be held tenderly and stroked and kissed. In some women, the area of skin above their kidneys is sensitive and they will respond with sighs of pleasure when it is caressed.

* * *

Still further above there is the belly, which should be caressed while the man's hand and mouth are travelling between the breast and the vulva. There are many places to linger a while, to kiss and lick and stroke and pinch. All this adds to the magic of the moment and increases the pleasures and the desires of the man and the woman.

* * *

The skin of the woman's arm pits is sensitive and the aroma there is exciting, especially when the woman is aroused and then a definite odor of femininity will exude from there. This odor will faintly resemble that of her vulva and its inhalation by the man will add to his excitation and ardor.

* * *

The back of the woman should be held and stroked and kissed, especially along the spine, which is the most sensitive area. It is thrilling to stretch a woman on her belly and then run your mouth and tongue up and down her spine and you will see her writhe with pleasure. Continue with this for a while and bite and nibble at her shoulders. Ah! how many places and ways there are to kiss and fondle a woman, and how endless the time seems when you are doing it.

*   *   *

A woman's neck is one of her most attractive features when it is slender and long and well formed and without blemishes. It is exciting to the touch and to the eyes when it is thus. The neck of the woman is very sensitive and the back more so than the front. A woman may sometimes go wild with delight if the back of her neck is bitten and kissed and sucked at. Her movement under the man or in his arms are sublime.

*   *   *

The head of the woman is full of sensitive spots and she will respond passionately when it is kissed and stroked. Her cheeks, her eyes, her brows, should be kissed and caressed, while you are murmuring fond words of endearment to her.

Blowing and nibbling on her ears or behind them will increase her passion.

*   *   *

The roots of the woman's hair are sensitive to the touch and she will respond with sighs of pleasure to the gentle stroking and pulling of her hair, as the man sinks his face into it and inhales its lush fragrance.

*   *   *

The arms, hands and fingers of the woman are a delight to hold and caress and kiss and nibble at. The inside area of the upper arm is the most sensitive and kissing and nibbling in that area will make the woman entwine her arms around you in great rapture.

*   *   *

Thus I have described in brief, but fully, the woman's body and how to arouse her, so as to make her into a ready and joyously willing and passionate partner, so that she may enter eagerly and breathlessly into copulation with you.

It is only thus that the man must approach the woman, for if she is unready or unwilling, approaching her will be like the ways of the beasts. It is only thus that the man can procure for himself and for the woman the highest and most ecstatic peaks of passion and the ultimate in pleasures and voluptuousness.

Unless the woman is ready and eager for copulation, it is a crime and a grave sin to try to mount her against her will.

Allah has decreed that only when a woman accepts a man freely, can he then enter her. If he forces her, he shall be cursed by Allah and his Prophet and shall be doomed into Hell.[27]

THE MAN

Allah has created the man to labour for his glory. He has given him a mind, which placed him far above the animals and He has made him different from the woman both in mind and body; in mind so that he can achieve and in body so that they can procreate and comfort and please each other.

*   *   *

Man is a thinker. He is a builder, an explorer and a scientist. He is also endowed with being positively and aggressively sexed. He is both a man and a male. Manhood is his human characteristic and maleness is his procreative characteristic. He is possessed with brains and hands to build and explore and fight for the glory of Allah and he is possessed of organs of procreation to copulate and impregnate the woman. The urge for copulation occupies only a part of his thoughts and dreams and it is a relatively minor part, except for those men who are so highly sexed that it is their only thought and pursuit and in these drives they are akin to women, and such men are useless to the Human Race, as they contribute nothing.

*   *   *

48

Throughout the history of Man, the woman has played a very major role in bringing delight and comfort to the man's body and heart, but she has played a minor role in the advancement of civilizations, because she is principally occupied with her body. At times, however, the woman played major roles in the destruction of civilization,[1] because she enticed the man towards full time use of his body with her, the man forgot his duty to Allah, and Allah smote him.[2]

* * *

The woman contributes much to making the life of the man easier and brighter and pleasurable by her softness and she brings utter delight to his heart by her magnificent responses in copulation.

* * *

It is not the object of this treatise to dwell on the man's various achievements, but rather it is to inform and instruct him on how he can secure for himself and the woman the maximum pleasure, in their relations.

Man has been endowed by Allah with positive organs of copulation, so that he may pursue the woman and finally subdue her and enter her after she becomes willing and eager to submit. In this pursuit, which in the civilized man is only symbolic, the woman will gladly submit if the man is attractive to her and she will derive great thrills and pleasure from the beginning of the chase until the time comes when she spreads her thighs and is penetrated, and then she will actively and passionately join in the act of copulation.

* * *

Woman, with her beautiful and soft body, acts as a strong magnet to the man. He is compelled by instinct and inclination to chase her, and she in turn desires that chase and provokes it actively with her charms. She is only momentarily subdued when she is mounted, but then she returns to passion in the man's embrace. In the end it is he who is conquered and subdued and captured, for she locks his penis deep in her vagina and his body is surrounded by her arms

49

and thighs and he is forced, by her movements and his, to discharge his fluids, and in this she fulfills her destiny.

*   *   *

By the chase and the subduing of the woman, in this case and in the wooing of her, the man must bring all of his finer traits into play. He will need tact, understanding, tenderness and certainly he must have full knowledge of the correct coital technique. The man must employ all these traits, even if he was to possess his humblest slave. For if he does not, he will have displeased Allah, and he will have descended to the level of the beasts, whose males corner the females which are in heat and quickly mount them, and after a few thrusts of their hindquarters, they are finished.

Alas, there are too many men like that.[3]

*   *   *

To attract a woman, a man must be pleasing of sight and smell and manner, otherwise she will be repelled and will derive no pleasure out of him.

The greatest satisfaction that a man can receive from the woman is the knowledge that he can satisfy and please her, while he is being gratified. This is the secret of true pleasure in copulation. The man can receive his maximum pleasures only when the woman is receiving her maximum pleasures and this will be mainly due to his effort and example.[4]

*   *   *

The Male Organs

Unlike the woman, who has all her organs of copulation and procreation inside her body, the man has his organs on the outside.

First, and the most prominent part is the penis (AL QAD-HEEB or AL AYR). I have given here only two of the most common names, but this organ has been given a thousand names in the erotic literature and these are mainly very vulgar and have no relation to its shape or true function.

50

The penis is the organ for copulation. It is also the organ for urination.

The penis is suspended between the thighs, being attached to the body under the pubic bone, and about five to six finger widths up from the anus.

There is only one orifice and one canal in the penis, and this is the pathway of both the urine and the seminal fluid, the latter being discharged during copulation, at the time of the orgasm. This canal, which is a round tube, stretches from the orifice in the head of the penis, which resembles a tiny mouth with lips which are oriented up and down, and continues and follows the underside of the penis, under the skin to the scrotum (AL SAFN).

In repose the penis varies in length and circumference with different men. The maximum size I have seen in my practice was a penis about the width of seven fingers in its length,[5] and it became monstrous in erection, measuring about the width of two and one half hands in its entire length,[6] and with the circumference of five thumbs.[7] This penis belonged to a very young and big Negro slave who was brought to me for examination.

I have observed that the biggest penises belong to the Negro Race (AL ZINJ), while the smallest belong to the Franks[8] (AL FARANJ).

* * *

At the base of the penis and hanging inside the scrotum, which is a bag made of very sensitive but tough skin that is overgrown normally with hair, the two testicles (AL KHAS-YATAYN) are located; these are two objects which resemble the eggs of large pigeons in shape and size, when the man is an adult. They are attached very loosely in the scrotum, one on the right and one on the left of the penis and they can be moved about rather freely inside the scrotum.

It should be noted with interest that the temperature of the scrotum is less than the rest of the body at all times. Why this is so I do not know. Perhaps the seminal fluid is better stored at this lower temperature and thus cannot spoil.[9] Only Allah knows for sure.

Also noted is that in a standing position of the man, one testicle will be seen to dangle lower than the other. In most of the cases that I have observed, the right testicle hung lower than the left. I do not know why this is so.

* * *

The greatest majority of male infants are born with their penises having around the head a piece of skin, which normally covers the head. In some this foreskin is very long and resembles a tiny elephant trunk, as the skin is wrinkled and with many folds. Rarely, an infant is born without this foreskin and thus he will require no circumcision (AL TOHOUR).[10] It has been ordained that all true believers should be circumcised and this operation is best performed before puberty(AL IBLAGH), as it will be much less painful.

Circumcision makes the penis cleaner. Otherwise material will always collect around the head, which will become very noxious.

* * *

It must be mentioned, although it is evident that the erection of the penis is essential for its penetration into the vagina, to deposit the seminal fluid (A'SA'EL AL MANAWI) which is produced by the testicles[11] and stored until it is discharged in a rush of pressure out of the orifice of the penis and into the uppermost parts of the vaginal canal. This happens when the man reaches his orgasm (AL SHABAQ).

Allah in His glory performs this miracle and it is staggering to the imagination, always, to realise how the beginning of a man or a woman is found in a few drops of fluid.

The seminal fluid is usually milky white in colour, although it could sometimes have a yellowish tinge and it has the consistency of mucus. Its odor is sweetish and very distinctive.

52

The maximum production of the seminal fluid occurs in boys who have reached the age of four to five years beyond their puberty, and at this age these boys may be capable of discharging in dreams, masturbation (AL ISTIMNA'A BE AL YADD) or in copulation, up to ten times a day.

Discharge through dreams (AL ISTIHLAM), occurs during periods of sleep and no dreams may be remembered, the only evidence being fluid-soiled night shirt or bed clothes.

*　　*　　*

As the man grows older, his capacity for multiple orgasms diminishes, but there are many variations in these frequencies between men of the same age. Some men's abilities diminish very quickly after a certain age, which is usually between middle and old age. Such men can perhaps experience one or two orgasms per week, while others may retain their ability to experience daily orgasms till well into their old age.[18]

*　　*　　*

However, with all men, to each his own time, and that I believe is written and predestined, there comes the moment when erection of the penis and the orgasm become no longer possible. Nothing can be done to remedy this and the condition will become the permanent circumstance of the man until his death.

*　　*　　*

There are times when erection will not be possible because of transient sickness or debility and this condition is temporary and sooner of later erection will return. Such episodes can occur in the young and old, but the young will recover much faster.

*　　*　　*

It is my thought that the permanent condition of impotence (AL U'NNAH) results from the complete drying up of the testicles, and the feebleness of the blood supply and pressure, and the atrophy of the muscles which raise the penis into erection.

*　　*　　*

In erection (AL INTISAB), there appears three types of penises in relation to their shapes, but without regard to their sizes, which vary from man to man.

*   *   *

The first type, which is most frequently found, is the penis which swells into the shape of a straight round rod.

*   *   *

The second type of penis is the one that will curve up-wards and towards the body when it swells and becomes erect. It will assume the shape of a gently curved rod, which will vary in its curvature from one sixth to one eight of the circumference of a circle. This penis is the ideal one for copulation because it fits into the natural curvature of the vagina.

*   *   *

The third type, which is relatively rare, is the penis that curves downwards and outwards, away from the body, and the curve may reach up to one sixth of the circumference of a circle.

*   *   *

Most women will find this type of penis difficult and some-times painful to accommodate in their vaginas.

*   *   *

I have seen a few penises which almost bend at right angles in their middle when in erection. In copulation, the unfortun-ate possessors of such tools can only insert the outer half into the vagina, and even that could only be done with great difficulty.

*   *   *

The head of the penis contains the orifice which is the gate of the exit of the urine and the seminal fluid.

Normally, there is a neck to the head, which in erection is thinner than the head. In erection the head swells and spreads flatly and a fold appears to surround its lower part, and the head and neck will resemble the head or neck of the hooded Indian snake, the cobra (AL SALL).

The skin of the head and neck is made of very thin and sensitive matter, which appears to be of the same variety as that of the vulva, the mouth and the anus. When this area is moistened and then gently rubbed and stroked by the woman, a feeling of great voluptuousness engulfs the man, and the sensitivity increases with the degree of excitation and thus with the state of erection of the penis.

* * *

When the man dreams of a woman or thinks of her or sees her, he will normally and immediately begin to have an erection of the penis. Without this erection, copulation is impossible. It is therefore evident that to copulate with a woman, the man must become erect of penis. Otherwise all his thoughts, dreams and passion will remain unfulfilled and in vain.

* * *

To procreate, a man must be able to become erect of penis and he must be able to instill his penis in the woman's vagina. He must then be able to sustain his erection until he ejaculates his fluid in the vagina. If he cannot sustain his erection to that point, and the penis is reduced in the meanwhile to its small unerect size, it will surely slip out of the vagina and it cannot be thrust back in until it becomes erect again.

The act of insertion of the penis into the vagina till the arrival of the orgasm in a very young man is very fast, and takes but a few thrusts of his buttocks. The man will usually recover quickly and he may be able to sustain another erection within the hour, and again a few thrusts will produce more fluid.

In such men, the act can be repeated several times in one day, perhaps up to ten times, but this is exceptional and cannot be kept up for many days.

* * *

As the man gets older, it will become harder for him to maintain his erection until he ejaculates. It will also take much longer for him to bring on another erection after he has ejaculated. The age is ultimately reached in every man when he becomes incapable of sustaining his erection for any appreciable length of time. Such men, who are usually old, may at times be able to sustain their erection for very short periods, but not until they ejaculate. Thus they may be able to copulate, but they cannot procreate and they will be wise to heed the saying of our great Prophet: "SEEK NOT THE FRUITS OF PASSION, IN WOMEN, IF YOU HAVE NO TEETH FOR IT."

*　　*　　*

I will now explain how the orgasm and ejaculation are produced in the man:

It can be seen that the first excitation produces the man's erection. Soon after, with the woman at his side, he will mount her and he will insert his penis into her vagina. His buttocks and the muscles of the abdomen and the other muscles all over his body will assume a state of tension. As he starts to move to and fro, in and out of the vagina, his state of tension becomes greatly aggravated and a point is reached very soon when the muscles cannot tense any more and cannot accept the state that they are in. Thus there is a sudden release of this tension. The result will be spasms of these muscles and those around the penis will push the fluid out of the scrotum, to the canal of the penis and into the vagina.

Why this is accompanied by exquisite feelings of pleasure is both a mystery and a blessing of Allah.

I must add here that the highest peak of pleasure is felt immediately before the start of the flow of the fluid from the orifice of the penis.

*　　*　　*

In the kingdom of the animals, copulation takes place only at special times and for very limited periods. During these times the female becomes ready for copulation by becoming possessed of a moist and well lubricated vagina, which will emit a powerful odor that will attract and stimulate the male into erection and it will seek to mount the female.

Once mounted, the female will stand still while the male thrusts his flanks to produce the orgasm. When this is accomplished, the male will immediately separate from the female.

The period of readiness of the animals for copulation varies with each species and it may last for a few hours or a few days, and the frequency of the return of these periods depends primarily on the length of the period of gestation of the species. Among the baboons, for instance, the female will retain a moist and ready vagina for about five days and during that time the male will mount her almost continuously, although it may only ejaculate but two or three times per day. If the female is not fertilised, it will come back into readiness in about one month.

At all other times, the males and females are oblivious of each other sexually, and it will be impossible for the male to mount the female even if it desires to. At such times, the vagina of the female will be completely dry and it cannot be stimulated into wetness. The female moreover will not stand still, but will run away when approached by the male.

During copulation of the animals, there seems to be no true awareness of pleasure, but only instinctive pawing, biting and thrusting, which resembles in action and noise, mortal combat.

*　　*　　*

NOTES

THE WOMAN

* FEE TAKWEEN AL MARA'AH WA A'RAJOL
1. Reference, no doubt, is made to the vows of celibacy which are taken by Christian priests, monks and nuns. The Prophet Mohammad has said: "THERE IS NO MONKHOOD (PRIESTHOOD) IN ISLAM."
2. This is an amazing statement for those times. The idea of the rights of women to complete sexual pleasure is fairly recent, even in Western thought and culture.

57

3. That happy, contented women have easy births if they have no physical or anatomical complications, became evident to modern medicine only very recently.

4. Labia Majora.

5. Labia Minora.

6. The process of ovulation and impregnation was apparently not clear to the author, otherwise he would have elaborated on it. Full knowledge of this was not revealed until the invention of the high-powered microscope in the 19th Century.

7. The fruit of the pomegranate tree (Punica Granatura) which grows wild in Iran and Afghanistan and surrounding countries of the Middle East. This tree has been in cultivation since ancient times. The fruit is round shaped and has a hard, thick rind, yellow-reddish in color, with a crown of sepals resembling a nipple. It is filled with seed, each surrounded by edible sweet or sour pulp. The tree is quite beautiful with scarlet flowers. In ancient times, the fruit was thought to have vermifugal properties.

8. It is still not fully understood why the color of the virgin's nipple and aureole changes after her defloration.

9. A genus (Gazella) of the antelopes and one of the most graceful and beautiful animals. It has lyrate horns and very thin and delicate limbs. Most of these animals inhabit the deserts of North Africa and the Middle East. They possess enormous eyes with soft expressions, which are thought by the Arabs to be most beautiful and the eyes of beautiful women are likened to those of the gazelle.

10. The recognition is made here regarding the ease or difficulty of birth, which depends on the width of the woman's pelvic structure.

11. Rickets is described here, which is mainly caused by the deficiency of Vitamin D. This was naturally not known to the author.

12. The Arabs of those times showed great preference for the sight of a big vulva and one which possessed a tight vagina. Their general taste in women ran to the rather stout, with wide hips and narrow waists, plump arms and legs and wide faces with big eyes and full pouting lips. They referred to a beautiful woman's face as resembling the full moon.

13. For example: The rabbit (AL ARNABAH), the cat (AL QUT), the starling (AL ZARZUR), the nightingale (AL BULBUL), and many others.

14. None, or very scant, attention had been given to the study of the change in character and color of the woman's organs and body during excitation and copulation, until Kinsey and later workers.

15. This illustrates the stress and the very high value that the Arabs put on the virginity of their women before marriage or purchase. The man who married or bought a woman on the understand-

ing that she was a virgin felt greatly cheated if she proved not to be one.

16. The practice is still prevalent in the rural parts of Egypt, also in the rural parts of the Sudan and other African countries. Not only is the clitoris removed, but also the labia majora and sometimes the labia minora. The object of this drastic and cruel operation is said to be to deprive the woman of feelings of sexual pleasure in intercourse so that they may not become promiscuous.

17. The author appears to suspect in a general way the homologous relationship between the penis and the clitoris.

18. The author is perhaps describing nymphomania.

19. Very perceptively, the author has recognized that nymphomania in reality is a mental disorder, which may lead to suicide.

20. A second name for the orgasm is given by the author, and it is HAZZAT AL JIMA'A, which means the quake of copulation.

21. The presence of the two Bartholin's glands was not known to the author, although he noted that secretions came from locations other than the vaginal orifice.

22. This practice (cunnilingus) is forbidden by Islam and is frowned upon by the Christian Churches. Several states in the U.S.A. and many other countries have codes which outlaw all mouth-genital contacts, even between married partners.

23. Most modern sexologists now stress the great importance of thoroughly stimulating the woman by the manipulation of her clitoris before coitus.

24. Although the Ancient and Medieval Arabs admired the physical beauty of the female breast, they did not put much emphasis on it as a very exciting and erotic part of the woman's body.

25. The Arabs were very much aware of the true artistry of the mouth to mouth kiss between men and women, long before the West discovered it. This is clearly shown in their literature since Pre-Islamic times.

26. The Arabs, after Islam, became very concerned with the cleanliness of their bodies, because it became mandatory for them to wash when water was available before every period of prayer and this is done five times a day. Thus, before approaching prayer, Moslem men and women have to wash their faces and necks, their arm pits, their genital areas and organs, their anal area and their feet. Their mouths must also be washed and rinsed.

27. This counters the malicious rumours which have been spread and which are still being spread about the status of women in Islam and it is told that the Moslem Religion delegates to women the status of a slave, at the mercy of man, and that she may be used against her will for his selfish pleasures.

THE MAN

1. The author no doubt refers to the Greek, Roman, Byzantine and Persian Empires, all of which declined mainly because of the decadence of their peoples, who became almost completely occupied with the pursuit of sensual pleasures.
2. Reference is made perhaps to the people of Sodom.
3. Alas! there are too many men like this today.
4. The author shows perception and genuine understanding of the conditions for an ideal relationship between men and women.
5. About five inches in length.
6. About ten inches in length.
7. A diameter of about two and one fourth inches.
8. All European peoples were called Franks, at that period.
9. The lower temperature is now known to be essential for keeping the sperm alive and motile.
10. The custom of circumcision is also practiced by the Jews. Now most pediatricians in the U.S.A. advise the parents to have this operation done to their boys, and it is performed a few days after the infant is born, while he still in the hospital with his mother. It is then a painless operation and the penis will heal very quickly. It has been noted that men who are circumcised almost never get cancer of the head of the penis. Moreover, women who are married to circumcised men rarely become afflicted with cancer of the cervix (the mouth of the uterus).
11. The author did not know that the fluid actually is produced by the prostate gland and that only the sperms are produced by the testicles.
12. Very few men are capable of such sustained performance after they reach their early thirties. Kinsey reports that from age 31 - 35, the average man is capable of three orgasms per week and this drops to two orgasms per week between ages 41 - 45. During ages 56 - 60, the average man becomes capable of attaining one orgasm per week only.

OF THE ARTS AND SCIENCES OF COPULATION[1]

"Copulate and propagate so that I shall praise you among the nations on doomsday."
THE PROPHET MOHAMMAD

By the grace of Allah, the man and the woman, in contrast to the animals, are endowed with the constant urge to desire and copulate with each other. The woman's vagina will always become moist and ready at the slightest stimulation of her lover. The man and the woman can then enjoy copulation for any length of time and this period will depend on the ability of the man to maintain his erection. And such ability is the one and only key to prolonged copulation and will result in prolonged excitement and pleasure for both.

* * *

Pleasurable fondlings and caresses of the man to the woman, and of the woman to the man, have no limit of time and can go on until one or both fall off exhausted. But copulation can only begin when the man's penis becomes erect and so long as he is beloved of the woman, she will always remain moist for him, even if she is in her menstrual period. (FATRAT AL HAYDH).

* * *

The man's and the woman's supreme and exquisite pleasures can only be brought about in copulation. Other kinds of pleasures can be obtained by manipulations and caresses, but full voluptuousness may only be reached in copulation.

* * *

Unfortunately the men who are uninstructed and ignorant in the arts of copulation cannot prolong the time from the moment that they penetrate the woman till they ejaculate. In reality, most men act like the animals and they cannot wait to mount the woman and after a few thrusts of their buttocks they will ejaculate, and are spent, and then they will roll over the woman and go to sleep.[2]

It is my observation that the woman achieves her highest pleasures only in copulation. If this is prolonged she can experience many orgasms of the most exquisite varieties and this comes from the release of the various tensions that build up during the application of rhythmic pressures by the penis, simultaneously on the clitoris, the outer and inner lips of the vulva, and orifice and walls of the vagina and the mouth of the uterus, and this together with the other tensions that are produced by the manipulations and caresses that the man bestows on her lips, breasts, buttocks and all the other sensitive areas of her body.

* * *

An orgasm of sorts can be brought upon the woman by the caress and the manipulation of her clitoris, and without copulation.[3] But this orgasm does not completely satisfy the woman and it will leave her in a state of some tension if she is not copulated with and brought to at least one orgasm thus.

* * *

It is my experience that the orgasm of the man, which can also be brought on by manipulation, becomes much more intense and voluptuous if it is delayed for hours in copulation. This is called The Withholding of the Orgasm (AL IMSAK AN AL SHABAQ).[4] In the end, when it is no longer possible or desirable to withhold, or if the woman has become utterly exhausted, the inducement of this orgasm will produce for the man indescribable pleasures and it will be a very long orgasm that will seem to go on and on. This is in plain contrast to the short, sharp and only moderately thrilling orgasm that is brought on by manipulation or after a few thrusts into the woman's vagina.

Another great and equally important satisfaction of withholding is the deep pleasure of the spirit that the man will experience when he becomes witness to the woman undergoing her many and violent orgasms, that will be possible only under his tutelage, and which will make her love him with great wonderment and passion.

With the man and the woman utterly spent after hours of such pleasures, they will become strangely refreshed in body and spirit and sleep will come quickly and sweetly and all worldly cares and sorrows will be forgotten and a new day will be faced with humble thanks to the Almighty Allah for his gifts of joy and tranquility and love.

*   *   *

Most men can reach the heights of perfection in the arts of copulation if they are able to keep their erection for hours. This will enable the woman to achieve one orgasm after another. It is my constant observation that the average woman will be able to attain as many as ten orgasms before she will become completely satiated and this may happen within a period of three hours in copulation.

*   *   *

With some women, who are not very healthy or robust, it is advisable to withdraw the penis after each of their orgasms, so as to let them rest, but then they may be mounted again and again.

Thus are spent nights of beauty and passion and the full potential of pleasure in the bodies of men and women is manifested and used, as Allah has created it to be used and appreciated.

*   *   *

I had pondered long on the ability of man to withhold his orgasm at will, and strangely the answer came to me when I was about thirty years of age and as a result of my observation of an animal that is found in great numbers in my native country of Yemen, which is the baboon (AL RABH).[5]

It had been known to me for a long time that the orgasm

63

of the man was brought on by the release of the tension of the muscles as I have described before. I knew that those tensions were aggravated by the rhythmic movements of the buttocks while the man was thrusting his penis back and forth in the vagina.

Since it was not feasible for me to observe different men and women in copulation, I turned to the observation and study of the baboons which are the closest to men in manner and structure. I had some captured and I kept them in a big cage in my garden.

My menagerie consisted of one male and three females and all were adults. Let me mention here that the baboon is one of the most active animals in copulation. The males appear to maintain almost constant erection and they will copulate almost continuously with the females which are in heat.

One day all the females in the cage were in heat, and I observed the male going eagerly from one to the other, mounting each for a few minutes and all the while maintaining a full erection.

The male would catch a female and then he would casually mount her and immediately start his thrusting, but he appeared to be very relaxed. When I would approach the cage he would watch me with keen interest and his eyes would follow my movements, but during all this time he would keep on with his thrusting and he would occasionally scratch his head and look around him very casually. A few minutes later he would dismount off the female and he would amble, while still in the state of erection to another female and he would mount her and again he would resume his casual thrusting into her. At one time, he noticed a cockroach on the ground beside him and he stooped down, but without dismounting, and picked it up and ate it with great relish.[6] Still he did not stop his thrustings.

Finally, after about an hour or more of this, during which he had mounted all the females several times each, he grabbed a female and mounted her. His body became more hunched and tense and his eyes glazed, and he became utterly oblivious to his surroundings and to me and his thrustings became quick and frantic. A few moments later he uttered a deep grunting sigh and his body trembled and his head dropped momentarily on his chest. He then dismounted from the female and I noticed that his penis was no longer erect. He had just had an orgasm.

The baboon would repeat this perhaps two or three times a day, but he would spend the rest of the day in his casual mountings and without orgasms.

*   *   *

Suddenly, that day I saw the answer in the actions of this dumb animal. The baboon was practicing withholding and thus he could continue almost constantly and all day in his copulation with the ready and moist females. His secret was obviously the state of relaxation in which he kept himself. When he desired an orgasm, he only had to tense himself and he would be spent in a few moments. It was as if he knew what he was doing.

*   *   *

I tried that same night what I had discovered. As soon as I mounted the woman who was my slave, I felt my buttocks tense instinctively, and I relaxed and I began my thrusts in a gentle but positive manner back and forth. Every time I felt my muscles tense up again. I relaxed and I felt myself drift away from the imminent orgasm, and thus I continued with my casual thrusts.

That night I was able to withhold for more than half an hour, and when my orgasm arrived it was the most intense and pleasurable and the longest that I had ever experienced. It was very much worth withholding for.

The woman had two intense vaginal orgasms, while previously, with my few minutes in her, she had only had clitoral pleasure. She was utterly thrilled and delighted and proclaimed that I was a new and a very exciting master to her.

*   *   *

65

AT MY ZENITH, I COULD WITHHOLD FOR MORE THAN THREE HOURS AT A TIME.[7]

* * *

And now I shall talk about the orgasms of women, which are many and varied. First I must stress that for procreation the man's orgasm is essential and no woman can conceive without it. All women, however, can conceive without achieving their orgasms and most of them do, because their men are spent after mounting them for a few minutes.

* * *

The woman does not discharge any special fluid when she gets her orgasm, as does the man, and as is wrongly thought by all people.[8] I believe that the discharge which is often seen and felt when the woman gets her orgasm is only the lubricating fluid that was produced by the vulva and the vagina during copulation, which collected in the vagina. This fluid is evicted out due to the contracting of the vagina during the orgasm. This is the truth about this phenomenon.

* * *

The orgasm of women varies in its voluptuousness from one woman to another and with the same woman at different times, and these variations depend on the man and what he does to the woman during copulation, and on how he does what he does. The feeling of the woman also depends on the amount of love that she feels for the man.

Of course, basically, the orgasms of all women are similar in that they are produced as a result of the sudden release of the tensions of their organs and muscles, but this release occurs at different times and for different reasons, even in the same woman.

The behaviour of women during their orgasms is of many varieties, as I shall recount. This will in fact prove what I have just postulated.

First I shall describe the orgasm which can be produced in all women by the expert manipulation of their clitoris and with or without copulation. This orgasm produces similar feelings in most women; it is the vaginal orgasm that is of so many varieties.

* * *

The clitoral orgasm (SHABAQ AL BADHAR) is produced by the stimulation of the clitoris.[9] Of course manipulating the other parts of the woman's body while caressing the clitoris will add greatly to her pleasure.

The time it will take to make the woman arrive at this orgasm naturally varies with the woman and her experience and depends on the man who is pleasuring her. Usually, this orgasm is arrived at very quickly and women bring it upon themselves by manipulating their clitoris, when in the absence of men.

To produce the most voluptuous orgasm of this kind without copulation, it is best to manipulate the clitoris with the mouth and tongue. This excites the woman and pleases her greatly, and it excites the man with the taste and odor of the vulva and this will help maintain his erection if he has any difficulty.

More than one orgasm can be induced thus, but it is thought best that the woman should be entered as soon as she has experienced it, and to work on bringing on one or more of the exquisite voluptuous vaginal orgasms.

However, if erection cannot be induced or maintained, then by all means produce a second and a third orgasm with your mouth and tongue, if that continues to please the woman and yourself.

The arrival of the clitoral orgasm is heralded by a sudden tensing of the buttocks of the woman and this is followed rapidly by sharp irregular intakes of breath. She will then move her buttocks back and forth very quickly, perhaps up to ten times and then all is over. It is strange that most women will seldom utter a cry during this orgasm, but a few will moan softly while exhaling.

* * *

The vaginal orgasm (SHABAQ AL MAHBAL)[10] is a complex phenomenon, and it is brought about only in copulation. The major area of feeling is in the organs of procreation, inside the woman. But pulsating voluptuousness will radiate to every corner of the woman's body. This orgasm may actually begin in the clitoris and then it will explode through the whole body. If the woman's breasts are being fondled or sucked, then the breasts will pulse with much feeling of pleasure. If the woman is being kissed in the mouth, then the orgasm will be felt by her in her mouth and tongue. Thus the degree of voluptuousness and the intensity of pleasure depends on the man, and what he does. The woman can only respond.

*   *   *

I shall now describe some of the orgasms that I have caused in various women. Memory still serves me well and I remember most of the truly passionate women with whom I have copulated. I still remember their names and I can still hear the silvery notes of their laughter. I can still remember their softness and the frenzy of their movements and their cries of exquisite pleasure during their passion.

Ah! but it is all memory now and soon I shall go to my Maker, and I shall thank Him for all the favours and blessings which He has bestowed on me and my loved ones during my long life.

The Savage (AL MUTAWAHISHAH)

Ameenah was a beautiful negro slave, whose color was that of ebony. She had a fine body and delicate features, and she walked with the stealthy glide of a stalking panther.

Her orgasms were wild and many, and when she was near her pleasure she would utter a low but piercing scream which went: "Ayeeeeee. . ." And she could clutch wildly at me. Her thighs would open wide and the rhythmic answering thrusts of her buttocks would stop. I could then feel her vagina start to pulse rapidly and she would heave deep breathing sobs and she would arch her back so that her breasts would become crushed against my chest. I would then take one of her breasts into my mouth and begin to suck at it vigorously and she would scream again and again, and she would shudder violently. At one time I approached her mouth to kiss it, and she bit me savagely on the lips, and I still carry the scar of that bite.

Ameenah's orgasms lasted to the count of about fifteen, and then she would fall quietly to relax with her eyes shut. Soon, however, she would resume the thrusting of her buttocks against me.

The Perpetual Mover (AL DA'IMAT AL HARAKAH)

Muneerah was a young Egyptian girl whom I took as my wife when she was about fourteen years of age. She was wide of hips and very slim of waist. She had long black shimmering hair and the complexion of fresh wheat.

She was a virgin when I married her, but it did not take me long to train her and she was a very apt student, who took quickly and joyously to the arts of love.

From the moment that I entered her, she would not keep still, and she would thrust and squirm continuously. Her orgasms came quickly and in rapid succession, and she would keep on with her movements, between the orgasms, and she would keep on uttering thus all the time: "Oh. . .Ah. . .Oh. . . Ah. . .Oh. . .Ah. . ."

Her eyes were always wide open, but unseeing as they were glazed and her vagina flowed copiously.

Withholding with her was most difficult. There are not many like her.

The Implorer (AL RAJIYAH)

Wardah was a girl from the mountains of Syria,[11] and her complexion was as white as milk.

She always tensed when I entered her and would not move, but she would wrap her arms and legs around me and never would she let go, and I did all the thrusting.

69

When one of her orgasms would arrive, she would loosen her grip and spread her thighs wide apart, and I could feel her vagina start to contract, and ripples of motion would go through her trunk.

She would begin to move her head from side to side and she would moan piteously as if she was in pain, and she would heave enormous sighs and repeat in a cracked voice: "Please......Please......Please......Please......" over and over.

I asked her why she spoke thus, and she replied that she was receiving so much pleasure that it almost suffocated her with its intensity and she was afraid that her heart would stop and she would die, so she was imploring me to stop my actions. Then she laughed impishly and said that of course she did not wish for me to stop, but to continue.

The Wondering One (AL MUTA'AJIBAH)

Zulafah was another girl from Syria and she had many charms and a heaving body, when in copulation. She enjoyed being kissed almost continuously and her mouth would be glued to mine from the moment that I entered her. Her long tongue would dart in and out of my mouth, and its odor was always very fresh, and her saliva was sweet to the taste.

Her hip motions in copulation were slow and lazy and her hands roamed all over my body.

Zulafah's orgasms would be ushered by an increase of the tempo and intensity of the thrusts of her buttocks. Her legs, which up to this time were held high and straight and very wide apart, would wrap around my flanks and her thrusts would then become very fast, almost frantic. She would then utter one long groan as her first vaginal convulsion overtook her, and then she would start to whisper hoarsely: "No. . . No. . .No. . .No. . ." and she would continue whispering thus until she was spent.

When I first asked her why she repeated the word no, she answered that in saying no, she meant that she could not

70

believe that any woman could experience such pleasures, and it always startled her and bewildered her into disbelief, when she was in her orgasms and for some time she could not decide whether she was awake or only dreaming.

Zulafah was a very sweet girl, and she was very easy to bewilder and please.

The Garrulous One (AL THARTHARAH)

Haneefah was a girl from Sanaa[12] in my native Yemen. She was small but perfectly formed and she had no flaws of skin.

She possessed an enormous vulva in comparison to her size, but her vaginal orifice was small and tight. I took her as my wife when she was about fifteen years of age.

She was a very quiet and shy girl and did not speak unless she was spoken to, and then she would answer very briefly, and with downcast eyes and in a very low voice.

She had a sweet nature and I loved her.

During our fondlings before copulation she would not speak one word, but she would caress me expertly as I had taught her.

When I entered her, she would become as a new person, and she would start to murmur the most pleasant endearments, thus: "Oh Master, I love you . . . Oh Master, please. . Oh. . Kiss me, Master . . Oh . . I am your siave . . . This is wonderful. . . Ah. . Ah Master," and she would continue thus all the while and the motions of her buttocks would continue to answer my thrusts.

At the start of her orgasm, she would stop her movements, and she would bring her thighs tightly together under me, and she would squeeze them rhythmically together, and she would speak again: "Ah . . . this heaven, Master . . . Ah . . . you are so good to me. . Ah. . Please. . Master, don't stop. . . . Ah. . Ah. . Ah fast . . . please, Master, fast . . No. . . Ah . ." and she would continue until she was completely spent. She would then spread her thighs wide apart so that I could pene-

71

trate deeper into her and she would always whisper happily: "Thank you, Master. . . Thank you."

Haneefah's orgasms were long and lasted up to the count of twenty.

The Thoroughbred (AL ASILAH)

Mansourah was a Bedu girl from Nejd.[13] She was about thirteen years of age when I married her. She had a bold look in her eyes and I taught her much.

I trained her well and she became magnificent in her voluptuous responses. She was like a thoroughbred mare which pranced and heaved and snorted under me.

When an orgasm overtook her, she would arch her back until she was supported only by her shoulders and the edge of her buttocks and I would have to take my weight off her. She would grow perfectly rigid and only her vagina pulsed and her body shook as with fever. But she never uttered a word and only breathed heavily and snorted. Her orgasm would be long and finally she would slump back exhausted and for a few minutes she would appear as if she was asleep. I would then kiss her mouth and breasts and she would revive and I would enter her again and she would start her prancing under me.

What a magnificent ride she was, and how voluptuous were my own orgasms in the end.

The Strange One (AL GHARIBAH)

Helena was a captive from the Island of Crete[14] and I bought her in Cairo when she was about twenty years old. She was stocky and very sturdy, with thick but smooth legs. Her skin was white and she had green eyes and a pleasant face. When she became pregnant I married her and she bore me three sons in all.

Thank Allah I was able to convert her to Islam and I changed her name to Fatimah, and she forsook her heathen ways forever. I am sure she is in Heaven now, for she was very devout.

72

In her orgasms she would hold me tightly and writhe under me, opening and closing her thighs spasmodically, and she would always murmur strange words and sentences in her native tongue. I would ask her what she had said, and she would reply always that she could not remember as she was in such ecstasy and she felt completely lost and could never remember what she said or did.

During her orgasms her vagina would tighten so hard momentarily that it would cause pain to my penis, but the vagina would relax again. Fatimah was very strange and wonderful in her loving and grasping, and I am sure that she adored me until the day she died.

The Hungry One (AL JA'IAH)

Hafeezah was the daughter of a physician with whom I was associated when I lived in Samarkand.[16]

She was about twenty-two years of age when I met her in her father's house. She was a widow, her husband having died the year before and she was still wearing her mourning dress. From the way that she walked and talked and looked at me, I sensed her smouldering passionate nature. She appealed to me greatly and excited me, and thus I asked her father for her hand. A week later we were married.

She had a small and delicate looking vulva, but her clitoris was large. Hafeezah proved to be insatiable in copulation and she practically jumped on me the first moment that we were alone.

Her orgasms were short, but very sharp and she would cry as if in pain, repeating over and over: "Ay. .Ay. .Ay. . Ay. .Ay. .Ay. .Ay. .Ay. .", and she usually went into her first orgasm very soon after I had entered her and she would gasp sharply and start thrusting violently with her flanks. When she was spent, she would slow her thrusting, but she never stopped her movements and very soon she would increase her tempo and another orgasm would overtake her and she would cry: "Ay. .Ay. .Ay. .Ay. . . .".

73

Sometimes, within the hour, she would have ten orgasms, and that was all the time that I could last in her.

At first I was delighted with her ardour, but soon her frenzy began to pall me, especially when I realised that I could never satisfy her, even if I continued to copulate with her for days, without any respite. I was sure that she would have been happy with any man who had a perpetual erection. Thus I divorced her after three months of marriage.

The Sobbing One (AL BAKIYAH)

She was a Frankish captive,[16] and I did not know her true name. I bought her in Damascus, where I was on a special mission to the Brother of the Great Saladin, and I named her Dhabyah.[17]

She was at least twenty years old and she had been a captive for about one year. She understood and spoke Arabic very poorly.

The woman was tall and big with a fine well shaped body. Her eyes were as blue as the sea and her hair was the color of straw, and it reached down to her waist.

Her face was wide and her lips were red and pouting and appeared ready for kissing, and her teeth were white and even. She was a delight to look at.

She submitted to me very meekly, but she was as cold as ice, and she did not give herself to pleasure. I was very gentle with her, although she excited me greatly, and she would not move or sigh when I mounted her. However, her vulva became wet from my caresses before I entered her. I kissed her on the mouth, but she would not open it for me and she refused to let me kiss her vulva.

One day, about two months later, I had mounted her and was at work on her for about an hour. I was determined that day to keep on until I dropped and I was in a tremendous state of excitation. I took one of her beautiful breasts in my mouth and I sucked at it vigorously and persistently. With both hands I lifted her buttocks upwards to allow her clitoris

74

to establish a firmer contact with the base of my penis and I increased the tempo of my thrusts into her. Suddenly she gave a gasp as if in pain, and I thought that perhaps I had bitten her without knowing it. I released her breast from my mouth, and I looked into her face, and she was staring at me with wide eyes, and suddenly enormous tears welled from her and she shut them tightly, and she took her arms which were lying limply on her sides and held me tightly. Her flanks started to answer my thrusts and her orgasms came, and she moaned and sobbed wildly, and she kept on sobbing and moaning until she was spent.

Her orgasm took a very long time to subside and I am sure it was more than the count of thirty. It was the longest orgasm that I have every witnessed in any woman.

When she was finished, I kissed her on the mouth and she opened it for me and allowed me to penetrate it with my tongue, but a few minutes later she turned her flushed face away from me and she fell into a deep sleep.

From then on she experienced regular orgasms in our copulation, but seldom did she have one as violent or as prolonged as that first one. However, she always sobbed after every orgasm and I was never able to make her tell me why. Perhaps in our copulation she always remembered a lost lover or husband who had given her as much pleasure as I was giving her. Or perhaps her pleasure itself made her sob because of its intensity.

She died one year later, from a grave illness.

The Tortured One (AL MUTA'ADHIBAH)

Lala was a Berber[18] slave who was given to me by the Emir of Fass,[19] in whose service I was for some time. She was very fair of skin, and big of body and her eyes were blue. When I received her, she was perhaps about thirty years of age, but she still looked young and she was strong and healthy.

While we were in copulation, I would be thrusting and fondling, and she would be with legs bent and wide apart, and with her chest heaving convulsive sighs, and she would start thus from the moment that I entered her.

Her orgasms were ushered by unnatural gruntings which were emitted from deep within her throat and she would appear as if she was choking, and her face would become almost purple in color. Her vagina would start to throb and her legs and arms would wrap around me, only to let go time and again.

Her gruntings and chokings would continue throughout her orgasm, which lasted perhaps to the count of fifteen or twenty.

Her orgasms ended abruptly and she would go into a faint during which she would be oblivious of everything. Her face would become very pale and her extremities would become very cold. Thus she would lie for a few minutes.

When I first asked her if she had felt any pain or discomfort she was surprised at my question, and said that, on the contrary, the orgasms produced in her great and indescribable pleasures and delights to the point where she could bear it no longer, and thus she fell into a faint.

After her orgasms she always felt greatly refreshed, and when she revived she would urge me in her sweet way to mount her and enter her again, and she would still be moist and ready for further pleasures.

      *   *   *

I have described but a few of the almost endless varieties of the orgasms of women, but I think that these examples suffice to illustrate my thesis.

Women are wondrous creatures, and they are a gift of Allah to us, and their reponses are a joy and a blessing. Allah in His wisdom has made them thus and each different from the other, so that men shall seek union with as many as they can, as each one shall bring forth a new delight.

If it was that all women were created alike in looks, temperament, and coquetry, we would soon tire of them, and the world would become depopulated in a very short interval of time.

      *   *   *

THE PREPARATION FOR COPULATION

You must approach copulation with much thought and preparation, if it is to be the act of man and not of the beasts. Only thus can true pleasures and delights be obtained for you and the woman, be she your wife, slave or lover.

*   *   *

Always, if possible, give the woman notice that you will be visiting her chamber, or that she must come to yours.[1] Thus she will have the time to wash and groom herself and make herself ready for your embrace. She will pay special attention to her vulva and she will remove all excess hair from her body. She will wash her hair and perfume her body, and thus make herself desirable and enchanting.

You too must wash and groom yourself. Your nails must be clipped and all the excess hair must be shorn from around your lips and your beard must be trimmed elegantly.

Both you and the woman must be dressed in fresh and loose robes, which should have no encumbrances and these should be very easy to slip out of, so that you may not fumble clumsily when the time comes to discard them.

*   *   *

Do not eat a heavy meal before you seek copulation, for this will make you sleepy and dull. Above all, avoid all the foods that may cause flatulence.

Have a bowl of fruit made ready, also nuts of various kinds, and perhaps a jar of honey and some fresh bread. With this you can start your time together by nibbling on and from which supply you can refresh yourselves later.

You should never partake from any spiced foods, as the spices will foul the smell and taste of your mouth and also will create an unwholesome body odour when sweating occurs during copulation.

Go forth with a clean and fresh smelling mouth. It will be

77

the first to be used when greeting the woman. Wash it thoroughly with soap and water, then rinse it with heavy rose water.

* * *

Greet the woman with a tender and ardent embrace and
always show by word and deed that you have selected her
because of your thought that no one else can give you as
much pleasure. This should delight her, as all women are
enchanted with flattery.

Sit with her for a while and engage in light and frolicsome
conversation. Women like to be wooed slowly and lightly at
first.

Caress her arms and neck and kiss her on the lips. If she
opens her mouth to you and darts her tongue into your mouth,
she is indicating to you that she ardently desires copulation
and you can proceed with the more serious gestures.

If, however, she does not open her mouth for your kiss,
she is still not in the mood for advanced dallyings.

Kiss her, fondle her, bring your hands into her chemise
and take her breast, and lower one hand to her vulva, which
should now be moist and almost ready.

When the woman's breathing becomes heavy, and she gets
more clinging, help her take off her robe and reduce yourself to complete nakedness and retire to the bed. Now she is
ready for the serious fondlings and ardent manipulations and
kisses.

* * *

Now explore her vulva and titillate her clitoris, while sucking at her breast, and fondle the other by pressing your chest
in a rubbing movement on it. Raise your face occasionally
to take her mouth into yours and suck at her lips.

Bring forth with your hand, some of the fluid from her
vulva to her breast and fondle it with your lubricated fingers.
This should give her a more voluptuous feelings, and the
taste and smell of the breast when you again take it into your
mouth should become more exciting to you.

* * *

I shall now give you the secret of success, if you are to give the woman and yourself the maximum of pleasures and voluptuousness which will make her ready and eager to be mounted and entered, and which will keep her pleasures and yours at their loftiest peaks during copulation:

ALWAYS STRIVE TO SIMULTANEOUSLY KISS, FONDLE, CARESS AND MANIPULATE AS MANY PARTS OF THE WOMAN'S BODY AS POSSIBLE.

This is the only secret, which together with your withholding, should bring you both to the highest sensibilities of the flesh.

* * *

When you are kissing the woman, do not just clutch at her body with clumsiness. With one hand you should fondle her breast and nipple, and with the other you should fondle her vulva and clitoris. Your body should not lay idle along the woman like a corpse, but it should be in constant motion against her body. Your thighs must rub at her thighs, even your toes must caress her toes. She should be taught to reciprocate thus for your pleasure. She must respond with her body, arms, hand and mouth, and not just accept your embrace placidly.

It is fortunate that most women, unless they are utterly unfeeling or idiots, need not be directly taught these things. When they see and feel the man expertly fondling them, they will respond by becoming experts at fondling him.

* * *

Descend now, and lightly nibble at the vulva and savour its taste and aroma. Suck at the clitoris and never keep your hands and fingers idle. With one hand or both, manipulate the woman's breasts. Once in a while remove your fingers from the breasts and let them roam lovingly and tenderly over the woman's body, from the neck downwards to any place that can be reached. Your hands and fingers must be in constant motion, and never stop for a moment, and this will

79

increase the woman's excitement and pleasure a hundredfold.

When you are caressing the woman's vulva with your mouth, it may be of more delight for both of you if she will also caress your penis with her mouth and tongue. This can be achieved in two positions. In the first, you will reverse your position in relation to the woman and you will squat with your head between her thighs while she will be lying on her back, and thus your buttocks will be positioned over her face. She can thus take your penis into her mouth.

Another variation is for both of you to be on your sides, but in the opposite directions. You will then be able to take her clitoris in your mouth, while she can take your penis into hers. Both your hands will be free to caress each other in any way that you wish.

* * *

This caress should bring you both, very soon, to the point of utter abandon, and it is a very pleasant diversion at times from the act of copulation and an excellent preparation for it.

* * *

Perhaps at times you may feel languorous and the wise and experienced woman will know what to do. She will lay you on your back, and she will prop your head and shoulders lovingly with soft pillows, and then she will commence to kiss you and caress you, starting from your mouth and going thence over all your body. Her hands and fingers and body will never be still. What wonderful feelings you will get and how sweet her movements will be.

Finally, the woman will concentrate on your penis and she will take it into her mouth, to nibble at and lick and suck. With one hand she will hold its length to caress, press and squeeze, and with the other she will hold and gently caress and squeeze the scrotum and testicles. She should be cautioned that these are very sensitive organs and that she must be very gentle and tender in their manipulation.

The woman's mouth and tongue will now be working at licking and sucking the head and neck of the penis and a feeling of delightful and tingling paralysis will seep all over your body and you will not be able to move.

During this caress, the woman could perhaps be squatting on her knees and with her vulva in firm contact with the shin of your leg which may be extended beneath her. Thus, while she is engaged with your penis, her vulva and clitoris may be stimulated by her weight and deliberate movements back and forth along your shin, and she may be able to produce her clitoral orgasm thus, and this will greatly add to her excitement and will bring her into readiness for the final pleasures when she must be penetrated.

The caress of the mouth to the penis should never be brought to the point of orgasm in the woman's mouth,[2] although some women may greatly desire that. Allah has intended for your fluid to be deposited in the woman's vagina, and when you feel yourself approaching your orgasm, you should ask the woman, gently, to stop and by all means hasten to mount her and penetrate her and if you find it expedient, practice your withholding until you must let go.

*   *   *

A very few women will be found who initially will be so shy and timid that they will become almost paralysed with fright when approached by the man for copulation. Much delicacy and fine behaviour is needed on the part of the man to initiate them, so that they may not be shocked into permanent repugnance.

Most any woman, after her initiation into copulation and when seeing the man caressing her vulva with his mouth, will herself begin to find great delight and excitement in the caressing of his penis with her mouth. It will not be only as a service to the man. The touch of the penis to her lips appears to bring her much pleasure both physically and spiritually and in this action she will be telling him in her very sweet way that she has joyously surrendered to him, and is thus paying homage to him in her surrender. There is no caress that is more intimate or personal or knowledgeable. It is a positive action

81

by the woman, in which she is indicating that she is participating willingly in bringing pleasure to the man, and not only yielding to him placidly and with passivity.

NO GREATER TRIBUTE AND NO GREATER DELICACY OF GESTURE CAN BE PRESENTED TO THE MAN BY THE WOMAN.

*   *   *

Yet, and because of initial shyness, the caress of the mouth to penis is the hardest to teach a woman. There will be women still who will not attempt it even after you have repeatedly caressed their vulvas with your mouth.

If you possess such a woman, beware of trying to induce her with spoken orders or by the abrupt reversal of your position when kissing her vulva, thus sticking your penis near her face. This will be a behaviour too crude and unworthy of you, and the woman will be repelled.

However, attempt at exciting her completely with all the fondlings that you know she enjoys. Lie side by side, facing each other and continue to caress and fondle her. Slowly and with great delicacy, lift your buttocks forward until your penis becomes on level with her breast. Take hold of it. and with the other hand hold your penis and direct it to touch the nipple and caress the nipple and aureole with the tip of the penis. Move the penis around to the other breast and to the valley between the breasts. Raise your buttocks once more and the level of the penis may now be near the woman's chin. It is a very rare woman, no matter how shy, who can resist the temptation now of giving the penis a nervous, shy and hurried kiss on its tip. Lower your penis and again caress her breasts with it.

To your delight and triumph, you may find the woman bending her face down to give the penis another kiss, only this time it will be less hurried and more ardent.

Soon you will find her going further down to take your penis into her mouth and her treatment of it will become more and more deliberate.

If the woman's mouth is engaged in kissing your body or mouth and she is caressing your penis with her fingers, let her moisten them with the fluid of her vulva and caress the penis thus.

This will give you a more voluptuous feeling.

* * *

When you and the woman have dallied and caressed as I have described, both will reach the point when you cannot wait a minute longer to hinder you from the union of penis and vulva, and thus you must mount her and enter her and start your sweet journey into the ultimate pleasures that are awaiting you.

* * *

May Allah be with you and may He bless you, and bless any fruit that may result from your union.[3]

THE ACT OF COPULATION

The act of copulation begins when the man mounts the woman and inserts his penis into her vagina. It is, in a sense, the final encounter between them, after they had prepared themselves and each other for it. This is the act that was designed by Allah so that the man may deposit his seed and fluid into the woman in order that she may conceive.

THUS COPULATION MUST BE CONSIDERED AS THE MOST NOBLE AND BEAUTIFUL AND MEANINGFUL OF ALL HUMAN ACTS.

* * *

Allah, moreover, has ordained that copulation must be an act of the greatest pleasure and He has equipped our bodies to feel thus. He has ordained that the man and the woman must enter into it willingly and joyously. Was not pleasure at the core of this act, men and women would ignore it. The

83

woman would be dry and the man would be without erection.
Thus the promise of pleasure must be in sight for both.

*　　*　　*

The animals in their copulation depend only on their instinct, as instilled into them by Allah. They are stimulated during very limited periods and their copulation is brief and with no conscious pleasure. The male will seek the female which is in heat and she will submit to him for a few moments, so that he may enter her.

They will then drift apart without further recognition or sentiment.

*　　*　　*

The man and the woman, on the contrary, to achieve all the pleasures that their bodies are capable of, must first employ their minds and hearts and spirits and later their bodies in their relationship. This is why Allah has allowed them and encouraged them to seek each other and copulate at will, without any limit of time and without restraints.

Aside from its prime objective of procreation, and which may take only one encounter to achieve, all other unions of men and women are made for the joy and the pleasure which are derived from these unions.

Allah be praised and thanked for that.

The orgasm of the man is the culmination of pleasure, and the temporary end of his ability to copulate. Immediately afterwards the man's erection will quickly subside and he will become impotent for a period which depends mainly on his age and physical stamina. His shrinking penis will then involuntarily slide out of the swollen and still ready vagina.

The orgasm of the woman, on the contrary, does not herald her inability for further pleasures, but rather it is a major episode in the act and it may be the beginning of a series of orgasms which will come in succession if the man is able to withhold his orgasm for some time. Thus an ideal

84

act of copulation is the one which lasts until the woman has achieved all the orgasms that she may be capable of.[1]

THIS CAN ONLY BE ACCOMPLISHED IF THE MAN CAN WITHHOLD FOR THAT LENGTH OF TIME.

*   *   *

I sincerely believe that the man can receive his greatest pleasures only in withholding, when he sees and feels the woman going through the extremes of pleasure in one orgasm after another, and thus reaching the heights of almost unbearable ecstasy. This should form the greatest part of his satisfaction and pleasure, which together with the actual feeling of voluptuousness brought on by the caress of his body and organs by the woman, will finally bring him, when he lets go, into a very long and magnificent orgasm of his own.

The man's orgasm, which can be produced after only a few minutes of copulation, produces very little satisfaction for the man and none for the woman. He will only feel a sense of failure for not being able to provide the woman with her pleasure. She will feel only tension and frustration and perhaps secret pity at his inadequacy, and he will become like a child in her eyes.

*   *   *

It brings no advantage to the man if he brings forth his orgasm simultaneously with the orgasm of the woman. There are ways by which the woman can deliberately heighten his pleasure and he can heighten her pleasures also during her orgasms.

But he must know what he will have to do. And if the man and woman are having their orgasms simultaneously, they will be clutching at each other and they will be oblivious of each other. They certainly will not be able to do deliberate things to each other.

THUS IT IS ADVISED THAT EACH SHOULD HAVE THEIR ORGASM SEPARATELY.

*   *   *

The man may increase many fold the woman's pleasures during her orgasm, if he will suck at her breasts. However, if he is having his orgasm simultaneously, he will not be able to do so, because he will be breathing hard and spasmodically and thus cannot suck.

There are many other actions which the man can do to the woman to heighten her pleasures and he can do that only if he is deliberate so that he will know fully what to do during that time.

*   *   *

The woman can increase the pleasure of the man when he is in his orgasm, but only if she, too, is deliberate in what she will do to him.

One thing she may do when he starts his orgasm, is to take his testicles in her hand and fondle them gently. At the same time she should press lightly with her thumb on the tube under the scrotum. This action will constrict the flow of the fluid and his pleasure will be intensified.

At the same time and with her other hand, she may clutch at his buttocks very firmly and spasmodically, and this too will increase his pleasure and prolong his spasms.

Or the woman may use both her hands and her fingers to rake at the man's back and she may kiss him or suck at his neck and shoulders with much ardour. This too will heighten his pleasure.

There are many other ways by which the men and the women can heighten each other's pleasure during their orgasms and these differ with different men and woman. They must experiement with their bodies to find them.

No man or woman can reach perfection in pleasure, which their bodies may be capable of, during their first, second or even their tenth union. However, soon the initial fumblings will be replaced by the more knowledgeable acts and finally each of their unions will become a poem of supreme and deliberate joy.

These are the unions which are blessed by Allah.

*   *   *

Know ye that the positions that men and women can assume in copulation are many and varied. However, some provide very brief and limited areas of body contact and are tiring to both, and thus are unworthy of serious study and attention.

I shall dwell in more detail on these positions which will provide the greatest comforts and pleasures.

The Movements In Copulation

The movement of the penis in the woman's vagina during copulation is certainly reciprocated by the movement of the vagina around the penis. This in effect shows that the relative movements of these two organs is the same. It is this movement in fact which stimulates the organs and, together with the accompaniment of the tensing of all the muscles concerned, will produce the orgasms of the man and the woman.

*　　*　　*

There are basically two types of movements and pressures of the penis and the vagina in relation to each other:

The first is the in and out movement of the penis into the vagina in what is a stroking motion, and the speed of the strokes or thrusts, will vary very greatly with the degree of excitation of the man and the woman.

The length of the strokes of this movement varies from the withdrawing of the penis almost completely out of the vagina, only to plunge it back to be completely engulfed up to the scrotum, to very short and quick strokes or thrusts with the penis deeply embedded in the vagina. This movement initiates the woman into her pleasures and will bring her forth to the brink of her orgasm.

The second movement, which produces extreme voluptuous feelings in the woman and may bring her into her orgasm, is a sideways motion combined with the forward thrusting. This in effect will produce a circular motion and it should be done with the penis deep inside the vagina, as deep as is can go, and the forward thrust should be of a very short stroke. The man must take care to keep the base of the penis pressed almost constantly on the clitoris and he must be able to feel the tip of his penis rubbing persistently at, and thus titillating, the mouth of the uterus.

Soon the woman will go into her orgasm and the man must keep up his pressure and circular motion of the penis until the woman is spent. He will thus insure that the woman will receive exquisite and almost unbearable pleasures and this will be due to the fact that all of her organs from the vulva to the deepest part of the vagina will be simultaneously rubbed during the orgasm.

It is a very rare and perverse woman who will experience no pleasure from such action, but there are a few such unfortunate women whose bodies and organs are completely without feelings.

The Positions of Copulation

The best positions in copulation, in that they are considered best because they will produce the most voluptuous feeling for the man and and the woman, are those WHERE THE MAXIMUM AREAS OF THEIR BODIES ARE IN SIMULTANEOUS CONTACT, AND WHERE THE MAXIMUM PARTS OF THEIR BODIES ARE ALSO AVAILABLE FOR EACH OTHER TO FONDLE, KISS, SUCK, CLUTCH AND NIBBLE AT. THE CIRCUMSTANCES MUST NATURALLY BE ALSO OFFERED WHERE THESE POSITIONS WILL INSURE THE DEEPEST PENETRATION OF THE PENIS INTO THE VAGINA AND WHERE THE BASE OF THE PENIS WILL EXERT THE MAXIMUM CONTINUOUS RUBBING PRESSURE ON THE CLITORIS.

Thus can maximum pleasures be obtained by the man and the woman for themselves and each other in the most delightful ways.

*   *   *

The first and most popular position of copulation is where the woman will lie on her back and the man will come to lie on top of her and facing her. His trunk will be positioned between her thighs, which she will spread to expose her vulva, thus enabling him to penetrate her.

In this position, the man must support himself on his elbows and knees, so that his weight may be kept off the woman, in order that she may breathe normally and be otherwise comfortable. Was it not for this support, this would be an impossible position to stage, especially when the woman is small and delicate. With the man supporting himself, however, the time limit for this position depends mainly on his strength and endurance.

The woman, to initially facilitate the entry of the man, should draw her thighs upwards towards her chest and as high as she is able to and with her thighs spread as far as possible. Later, when the man has entered her, she may bring her thighs downwards and wrap them around his flanks and she may rest the balls of her feet on his buttocks, thus relieving the strain which may be present on the muscles of her thighs due to their spreading.

It can be visualised that this position does not allow the man complete freedom of movement because his arms are half locked at the woman's sides and he can move them freely only from the elbows to the finger tips. However, he may temporarily support himself on one elbow and he will thus have the complete freedom of one arm at a time.

If this position is to be sustained for any length of time, it is essential that the mattress lain upon be firm but soft, otherwise pain will soon seep into the elbows and knees of the man, and he will be robbed of any prolonged feelings of excitement and pleasure.

This position affords many pleasurable contacts of the man and the woman. Their bodies will be in constant touch and friction. The man's chest will cover the breasts of the woman and by moving his chest from side to side deliberately over the breasts he will rub the nipples with his flesh and this will increase her feelings of excitement and pleasure.

The man's mouth is positioned over the woman's mouth and they may engage in kissing of the most ardent nature in each other's mouths, or in any place that their mouths can reach, thus increasing each other's frenzy and passion.

If the woman is not too short, the man may easily bend his head downwards and take one or the other of her breasts into his mouth, and this should add considerably to her pleasure, especially during her orgasms. If the woman is too short, the strain on the man's neck will be too much for any prolonged action at the breasts.

The man's free arm, when he is supported by one elbow, can roam all over the woman's body, and he can reach her thighs and calves and all the other parts, which will be ready and tingling to receive his touch.

*   *   *

THE MAN SHOULD NEVER BE STILL EVEN FOR A MOMENT. HIS MOUTH AND ARMS AND HANDS AND BODY AND PENIS SHOULD ALWAYS BE IN MOTION. HE MUST ALWAYS BE KISSING, CARESSING, PINCHING, KNEADING, NIBBLING AND THRUSTING. THUS WILL THE WOMAN BE KEPT INFLAMED AND SHE WILL BE HASTENED TOWARDS HER ORGASMS.

When any of her orgasms arrive, the man must know what to do to increase and prolong her pleasure.

*   *   *

When the woman is temporarily spent, the man must not immediately remove himself off her body, but he must keep on with his thrustings and fondling and kissing and he must do this more gently now, so as to slowly bring her back to normal sensations. He must kiss her and whisper sweet endearments to her. She will be happy with him and she will gratefully enfold him again with her arms and thighs.

*   *   *

If the woman is fragile, it may be best to get off her after each of her orgasms and to lie by her side, so as to give her some respite, and she should be caressed in a very gentle manner. A little later she will indicate by her revived actions, and in ardent ways, that she wishes to be mounted again.

Many women will go from one orgasm to the other without desiring for the man to remove his penis, or to give them a rest. On the contrary they seem more inclined to continue to be highly excited between their orgasms.

The limit for such manner of copulation will be the final exhaustion of the woman or the inability of the man to withhold any longer.

When the time comes for the man to have his orgasm, the woman who is well trained will know what to do. In this position her arms, hands and mouth are available to do such things as will heighten and prolong his pleasurable spasm

*　　*　　*

There are two principal variations of this first position. One is for the woman to lift her legs and to place them on the man's shoulders. For this, the man must raise himself from his elbows and must support himself with his hands.

The woman's vulva is now greatly elevated and the penetration of the penis in its full length and thrust forward, will be to its maximum into the vagina. This position is not very comfortable for either the man or the woman, especially for the woman, who may develop pains or discomfort from the very deep thrusting into her. However, some women derive great excitement from the feeling of the penis going very deeply into them.

*　　*　　*

The other variation is even more extreme, and it is where the woman will bring her legs upwards and as much as possible towards her shoulders, so that she may become almost doubled up. This will raise her vulva even higher than before, but the available length of the vagina will be drastically reduced, and this will make the peneration of the penis into it more uncomfortable.

*   *   *

These variations may be tried as a matter of temporary diversions. The only advantage offered to the man is to afford him an excellent view of the exposed vulva, where he can actually watch his penis go in and out of the vagina and such sight could add considerably to his excitation. However, here, neither the man nor the woman can fondle or kiss each other, for they are always separated by her thighs.

*   *   *

Another position of copulation is where the man and the woman approach each other face to face, by lying on their sides.

Here, the woman will lift her upper thigh and bend it upwards to separate her legs and expose her vulva and the man can then enter her. Her thigh may now rest on the man's flank.

This position does not offer the deepest penetration into the vagina, but it is adequate, especially if the penis is long and if the woman cannot tolerate any kind of weight on her because of extreme fragility, illness or because she is with child.

The man may assist the woman in making this position much more pleasurable by the manipulation of her clitoris with his fingers and thus he may hasten her towards her orgasms. His hand will also be free to roam on her flanks, thighs, buttocks and breasts, which latter he can easily take into his mouth.

Kissing on the mouth is possible at all times from this position and this adds greatly to its assets.

The woman, in turn, will have her upper arm and her hand free to caress the man on his body. She can reach his scrotum and testicles with her fingers and, when he nears his orgasm, her caresses may become more deliberate and pleasure heightening.

With the other arm, which will be under her neck and around her shoulders, the man can also caress the woman and he will be in the position to bring her to a more clinging and ardent embrace at the times of her pleasures.

Variations in the postures and positions of the legs of the man and the woman can be tried for the best in comfort and intimacy.

Corpulent men and women, and women in the advanced stages of pregnancy will not benefit from this position, except as they are resting from copulation. In these cases, penetration of the vagina by the penis will either be impossible or very shallow and inadequate.

*   *   *

The third position where the man and the woman face each other is when the man sits down on a low stool, with his back in an upright position and the woman will come forth and sit deeply in his lap and her legs will be spread apart and around his waist. Thus her vulva will be vulnerable and she can be easily penetrated by the man's ready penis. In reality she will sit on his penis, which will then slide upwards and deep into her vagina, as she is settling on his lap.

The woman can then wrap her legs around the man to suit her mood, or she can let them down to be supported by the floor. If her legs are too short and her feet will not reach the floor, foot stools will have to be supplied for her. Thus she will have the freedom to move up and down against the man, while enfolding his chest with her arms, and her movements can be deliberately planned by her to suit her pleasure. This is desirable because the man here has but limited opportunity for full thrusting, unless he will hold his weight by his hands with which he must clutch the edges of the stool. But this will not be conducive to maximum pleasure, as his arms and hands will thus become unavailable.

The deepest penetration that is possible in any position, may be achieved here and both the man and the woman will find this very wildly gratifying. Their arms, hands, trunks and mouths are free to caress and fondle each other's, and the man is moreover able to suck at the woman's breasts.

The movements that can be practiced in this position will produce the most exciting and voluptuous sensations in the woman, because she can move up and down, to make penetration into her as shallow or as deep as she may desire. She can also move sideways in a circular motion to add to her pleasures. Moreover, her clitoris will be under almost constant pressure and friction from the base of the man's penis if she wants to keep it that way.

The times when copulation from this position cannot be comfortably practiced are when either the man or the woman are too corpulent, or when the woman is in the very advanced stage of pregnancy.

*   *   *

It may be an inducement to greater intimacy if the man and the woman will often engage in the fourth position of copulation, where they will also be face to face. This position will hold many pleasant surprises for both.

Here, the man will lie down on his back and the woman will come and lie on top of him. She will spread her legs and drape them on his sides and thus she can easily be penetrated by his penis. This, in effect, is the reversal of the first position, where the man mounts the woman. Here, she mounts him.

Such a position is actually a delightful change. The woman, now, will possess complete freedom of her actions and movements, as she is not pinned down by the man's body. The man, in turn, will be relaxed and comfortable and the woman does not have to support herself on her elbows and knees. She is so light and her weight on top of him must only add to his delight.

The woman is free from any strain and she can abandon herself to any lascivious movements and gyrations to suit her mood. She can move in all directions and she can stimulate every organ, and at the same time she can caress and kiss the man and her earnest attentions will bring great excitement to him. He, in turn, will have his arms, hands, legs and mouth free to use on her. He can move his buttocks either with his own rhythm, which the woman will answer or he can answer her own thrusts.

The man can lift her temporarily off him, by holding her by her arm pits and he can kiss and suck at her breasts, which should further immerse her in a whirlpool of delight.

This position is perhaps very suitable when the woman is still new to the arts of copulation and giving her the freedom to move and act as she desires will quickly acquaint her with the requirements of her body in pleasure. It will also eliminate her shyness and modesty in no great time.

When the man feels indisposed or tired, it is wise to use this position and thus to let the woman do most of the work. Where the woman is fragile and cannot tolerate any kind of weight on her body, this position is recommended without reservation.

*   *   *

While the woman is in position on top of the man, she may bend her knees along his sides and thus she will be able to straighten upwards and the man's penis will remain in her vagina. She can now move up and down and in a circular motion around the penis, which will be deep in her.

The woman, however, will be away from the man and she can only bend forward towards him very slightly, if she prefers to keep his penis inside her and she will not be able to kiss and fondle him, except from far with her hands. The man can lift his trunk up and support himself with his hands or elbows and he will be able to take her breasts into his mouth.

This cannot be a very satisfactory union for either the man or the woman, because their bodies will not be together. It may be practiced at times, however, to experience new sensitivities.

*   *   *

95

At other times and to enjoy frolicsome variations, copulation can be tried and achieved in other ways than with the man and the woman facing each other. There are certain circumstances also which may make face to face copulation impossible or inadvisable.

In such cases there are other positions where the woman can be approached from behind, and which I shall describe.

*　　*　　*

The woman can be entered from behind if she spreads her legs apart to expose her vulva. She can be standing up, but she must bend her trunk forward. Or she can be on her hands and knees on a bed or divan. When the man penetrates her, he may hold her by her waist to control his thrusts into her.

Penetration of the penis can be deep. However, very few women will derive much pleasure from this position, because their bodies will not be engulfed or embraced by the man. The woman cannot kiss or caress the man, but must submit to his thrusts with her back turned to him like an animal.

Here, the man can help the woman in bringing forth some additional pleasures by bending forward and fondling her breasts with both his hands, or he may bring forth one hand to fondle the clitoris.

The man may reach the woman's neck and shoulders to kiss them and suck at them with his mouth and this may give the woman an added thrill.

This is a favourable position when the woman is in the advanced stage of pregnancy or if she is corpulent. If the man is corpulent and with a protruding belly, this position may be his only recourse in copulation, because his belly will fit above the woman's buttocks.

*　　*　　*

The man and the woman can lie down on their sides with the woman's back towards him and he can raise her thigh and enter her.

This position is the most restful and satisfactory for the

woman who is heavy with child or who is very sickly. In the former case, deep penetration will not be possible because of the position of the child. However, it will please her greatly to have at least some of the man's penis inside her. He may very carefully caress her swollen breasts and perhaps her clitoris, while kissing her back and shoulders and neck. She will be happy because she will know that she is still desired even in her unattractive and bloated condition.[2]

I must caution here that the woman should not be approached in copulation after the end of her seventh month of pregnancy.[3] Such union after that date will benefit neither her nor the man. She in reality will have become too gross both in body and temperament to allow for a joyous occasion.

*   *   *

There are many other positions from whence the man may enter the woman. However, all are not worthy of mention because much strain is involved, thus robbing them of the opportunity to bequeath pleasure, especially for the woman.

In most of these positions the woman is only used and sometimes abused, rather than given the opportunity to willingly and joyfully give of herself and for herself the rightful pleasures that are her right, by the grace of Allah.

*   *   *

Before her defloration (FADH AL BAKARAH) the virgin is as innocent of the true and voluptuous pleasures as a new born infant. It is the man who opens this gate for her, and hastens her into the garden of delights. Her entry may be of shy and delicate passion or it may be painful and shocking. The man's manner when he deflowers her will determine which it is to be.

The defloration is the most important and critical event in the woman's life, for it may influence her whole future response to the man both physically and spiritually. It may be that physically, some repair may be effected following damage done during the defloration act itself and the woman

97

may ultimately come to respond with some pleasure. But she will never forget nor forgive the man who by his uncouth behaviour caused her great physical pain and spiritual anguish while occupied in her defloration.[4]

It must always be remembered that the virgin (AL ADHRA'A) may be profoundly shocked or frightened by the sight of the man's erect and swollen penis and it behooves the civilized man not to expose it suddenly and flagrantly to her view.

Much time and patience may be needed between the first encounter with the virgin and the moment when he will introduce his penis into her. During this period, the virgin must be put completely at ease and she must be prepared with gentle and sweet words and caresses, so that her vagina will become moist and ready, instinctively, to accept the penis.

THIS ACT MUST BE ACCOMPANIED WITH THE GREATEST OF CONSTRAINT.

* * *

The most natural position for defloration is where the virgin will sit on the man's lap, facing him, and thus she may be coaxed gently to spread her thighs when the time comes and to descend voluntarily on his penis.

The virgin, like all children, has been accustomed to sit from infanthood on the laps of her male elders, to be hugged and kissed, and this position will not cause her undue embarrassment or anguish, while she may come to feel panicky and may even become hysterical if the attempt is made to lay her on her back, and to pin her down and mount her.[5]

Time must be taken, while the girl is sitting down on the man's lap to make sure that she has become soothed and perhaps aroused by the gentle fondling of her body.

When it is felt that she has become ready to be entered, then she should be instructed with great delicacy to straddle the man, and to descend on his penis, which he should position for her with his hand. She must be assured that this operation will hurt but very little, if at all, and only initially.

She must be told that she is free to stop her descent if she starts to feel any pain. She may be told in a playful manner that she may close her eyes if she feels too shy.

As soon as the man feels his penis start to go through her hymen, he must hold her tenderly but securely and he must ease her down with positive pressure, so that the penetration of his penis will be effective and complete. All this while, he must continue to whisper sweet words of endearment to her and he must continue to fondle her gently to keep her aroused.

The man must not now start with his thrustings, but he should remain still, to let the girl savour the new feeling of his penis in her vagina. Once he ascertains that she has become at ease and is suffering from no pain or discomfort, he may start with very gentle thrusts.

THUS THE NEW WOMAN IS INTRODUCED INTO HER PLEASURES.

*   *   *

Contrary to the taboos (AL MAMNOUA'AT), I find no harm at all in copulating with the woman who is in her menstrual period (FATRAT AL HAYD).[6] However, such copulation should not be attempted on the first day because of the copious nature of the bleeding.

I have observed constantly that women possess much stronger desires for copulation when they are in their menstrual periods, and they will seek it avidly if they are propositioned and their pleasure will arrive very quickly and will be breathtaking in its length and intensity. But I do not know why this is so.

However, only enter into copulation with the woman whose blood does not have a foul odour, for this will indicate that it is putrid and it may seriously inflame your penis.

After withdrawal, always wash your penis immediately with plenty of soap and warm water, to avoid the irritation which will surely afflict it if the woman's blood is allowed to stagnate on it.

*   *   *

Once you and the woman has become completely satiated in copulation, do not just roll off her like a lump of dead flesh and go to sleep. But keep her in your arms and caress her gently and with tenderness and murmur sweetly in her ear, until you both go to sleep together.

THUS IS LOVE ASSURED AFTER THE PASSIONS ARE ASSUAGED.

NOTES

CHAPTER TWO

1. FEE FOUNOUN AL JIMA'A WA OULOUMEH
2. It is reported by Kinsey that about three-quarters of all men reach their orgasms within two minutes after the initiation of copulation and a great many of those will arrive at their climax within less than a minute, or even within ten or twenty seconds after penetration into the woman.
3. Freud, unlike Kinsey, believed in the existence of two distinct and different orgasms in women, one clitoral and the other vaginal.
4. Kinsey reports that only a minority of men would consider the acquiring of a withholding ability as a desirable substitute for direct and rapid copulation.
5. The baboon is a monkey which inhabits many parts of Africa and Asia. It belongs to the genus CYNOCEPHALUS and it has a dog-like face and a red rump. The fore and hind limbs are of equal size, thus permitting a quadrupedal giant. In Yemen, the baboons are of medium size, with the males reaching a weight of perhaps up to sixty pounds. They live in rocky cliff country in colonies of various sizes reaching into the hundreds and they are a serious economic threat to the farmers, owing to their destructive raids on the corn and grain fields and orchards.
6. The baboons are omnivorous and will eat insects and small animals, as well as plant matter.
7. Kinsey considers it too demanding and abnormal if the man tries to withhold for ten to fifteen minutes in copulation, in order to wait for the woman to arrive at her orgasm. This is the time that he estimates which may take the adversely conditioned woman to arrive at her climax.
8. That the woman discharges special fluids during her orgasm,

100

as does the man, has been a long accepted fact since very ancient times. However, recent studies by Kinsey and others have shown that in reality, this is not the case and it is as described by the author.

9. Freud maintained that the climax produced by the manipulation of the clitoris alone is a phenomenon of childhood sensation.

10. Freud concludes that when the woman finally engages in copulation, the clitoris will become stimulated during intercourse and its role is to conduct the excitement to the adjacent genital parts; it acts like a chip of wood which is utilized to set fire to the main fire wood. Freud adds that this transference often takes time to be accomplished and during the transition the woman remains anaesthetic to all feeling of pleasure in her vagina.

11. The author used the old name of Syria in his manuscript: BILAD AL SHAM, and this name probably covered the area of what is now Lebanon, Palestine, Jordan, in addition to the present area of Syria. Damascus, which was the capital of the Ummayad Kalifate (661-749 A.D.), is still the captial of the present day republic of Syria.

12. Sanaa is a town in central Yemen and it is the capital of that country. It is a very ancient city, which now has a population of about 50,000. The elevation is a healthy 7000 feet above sea level. Yemen was an absolute monarchy, ruled by Imam Ahmad Hamid Al Deen. However, a week after he died in 1962, a revolution broke out, and a republic was proclaimed and established, with the help of Egyptian troops. The son of the Imam, Al Badr, who was proclaimed Imam when his father died, fled to Saudi Arabia and is still reported to be there. The Egyptian troops and administrators pulled out of the country in November of 1967, but civil war still rages on between the Republican army and the Royalist tribes, who still hold much of the countryside, under the leadership of the princes who are the cousins of Al Badr.

13. The Nejd is an area lying between the central and north central parts of the Arabian Peninsula. It is composed of desert plains and arid mountains and a few oases. The majority of the inhabitants are nomads (BEDU). The Nejd is now part of the Kingdom of Saudi Arabia.

14. Crete is a large island in the Eastern Mediterranean Sea along the south edge of the Aegean Sea and about 150 miles south east of Greece. The Island was occupied by the Arabs in 823 A.D. In 1204 A.D. it was conquered by the Crusaders and was granted to Boniface, the Marquis of Montferrat, who sold it to the Republic of Venice. It is now an integral part of Greece.

15. Refer to previous annotation on Samarkand on page 10.

16. She must have been a European girl who came with the Crusaders to the Near East. During those times all female captives were

101

sold into slavery, and both the Arabs and the Crusaders engaged in this cruel practice.

17. A female gazelle.

18. The Berbers are a Hamitic speaking people ranging over North Africa southward to Senegal, forming three fifths of the population of Algeria and a much larger proportion of the people of Morocco. The invasion of North Africa by the Moslem Arabs between the Seventh and Eleventh Centuries A.D. drove them inwards into the Atlas Mountains and imposed on them the Moslem Religion and the Arabic Language, and thus in time they became largely assimilated with the Arabs. Many of the Berbers have blue eyes and light-colored hair, and there is a widely accepted view that they are closely related to the Caucasoid people of Europe. The Tauareg or the Blue Men of the Sahara Desert are Berbers.

19. A city in northwest Africa, in Morocco, lying 95 miles east of the Atlantic Ocean and 85 miles south of the Mediterranean Sea. The old city was founded by Idris II in 793 A.D., and it has a present population of about 250,000.

THE PREPARATION FOR COPULATION

1. In those times, the houses of the upper classes were divided into many chambers and apartments and the man who was the head of the household had his own private apartment, where he lived alone. Each of his wives and their children also had their own apartment or chambers, and his women slaves occupied their own separate quarters. Thus when the man wanted one of his women for the night, he would send word for her to come and spend the night with him in his chambers. When a woman was a great favorite, and without children, the man would sometimes go and visit her in her own chamber, and perhaps spend the night there, and this was considered by her as a great honor and a sure sign of his love.

2. Although the author had been extremely liberal in advocating all manners of caressing, he has set this limit to normal behaviour, which is very logical because if this caress is brought to its finality with the man ejaculating in the woman's mouth, nature would not be served. The author's advice is always for the man to impregnate the woman as God has intended, and no procedure for birth control is mentioned in the book.

3. The author here reveals his philosophy, which does not call for promiscuous behaviour as some may have concluded, but rather for the unions of men and women to be in accordance with the precepts of Islam, and thus he calls on God to bless all the children (legitimate) that are born as a result of these unions.

THE ACT OF COPULATION

1. Most modern sexologists now agree that the normal woman is capable of achieving multiple orgasms if she is stimulated properly and for a long time in copulation.

2. Great compassion and understanding of female psychology is demonstrated by the author.

3. This is very good advice. All obstetricians and gynecologists today caution against copulation with the woman after the end of the seventh month of her pregnancy.

4. Great perception is shown by the author, regarding the psychology of the virgin's attitude to her defloration and the stress that he puts on restrained action by the man cannot be passed over lightly or ignored.

5. During those times, most girls were given in marriage when they were mere children in their early teens and they received no sex education, but perhaps only inadequate and hurried instructions by their mothers and other female relatives on their wedding day. Thus what the author describes is understandable.

6. Copulation with the menstruating woman is forbidden in Islam, in accordance with the following verse of the Holy Qur'an: "AND WHEN THEY QUESTION YOU CONCERNING MENSTRUA TION, SAY IT IS A HARM, SO LET WOMEN ALONE AT SUCH TIMES AND DO NOT GO IN UNTO THEM UNTIL THEY ARE CLEANED. AND WHEN THEY HAVE PURIFIED THEMSELVES, THEN GO IN UNTO THEM AS ALLAH HAS ENJOINED UPON YOU. TRULY ALLAH LOVETH THOSE WHO TURN UNTO HIM, AND LOVETH THOSE WHO HAVE A CARE FOR CLEANLINESS."

OF THE ABERRATIONS AND MORBID CONDITIONS OF MEN AND WOMEN[1]

"And Lot! Remember when he said unto his folk: Will you commit abominations such as no creature ever did before you?

THE HOLY QUR'AN

THE ABERRATIONS OF MEN AND WOMEN

PERHAPS due to the sins or to certain weaknesses of their parents, or due to other mysterious causes known only to Allah, some infants are born who are neither complete males or complete females. These are the hermaphrodites (AL AKHNATH).[2]

* * *

For instance, an infant may be born with a very small penis, and he may have one testicle or none in his scrotum. There may be a small and underdeveloped vulva under the scrotum. When the child matures, his penis will remain very little and his hips may widen and assume the female form, and he may develop breasts.[3] Such men naturally cannot marry because they will be impotent and they may be intensely attracted to men.

There are infants who are born as females and who will possess normal vulvas. However, when they grow to maturity. their bodies will not develop the soft contours of women, but rather the hard muscular shapes of men. Their voices may become deep, and they may sprout hair on their faces. Their breasts will not develop and their clitorises may grow to enormous sizes.[4]

They will usually have no inclination towards men, but may feel strongly attracted to women.

There is nothing that can be done to change these creatures into normality, and prayers to Allah to make their lives as easy and as bearable as possible are the only recourse.

It is hoped that they may finally be delivered into Allah's grace, so that He may allow them to establish their true identities in the Hereafter.

* * *

There are physically normal men who for some unknown reasons wish desperately to become women[5] and likewise there are some completely and exquisitely formed women who are perfect and lovely in every detail, who wish to be men and they abhor their femininity.[6]

The men may be found occasionally dressed, and very charmingly, in women's clothes and in their homes they will indulge in feminine activities such as cooking, sewing and taking care of babies and little children.

The women, on the other hand, may forsake their dresses and they will attire themselves in the garb of men. They will engage in the sports of men, such as riding and hunting and many will go on military campaigns, disguised as soldiers, where they usually distinguish themselves as brave and ruthless fighters. History books are full of tales of such women.

* * *

I was once approached by a perfectly formed man who wanted me to castrate him and construct a vulva for him. He said that he would give anything to be able to become a woman, so that he could bear children and suckle them.

Naturally, I told him that I could do nothing for him.

* * *

It is known with certainty that some men copulate with animals, such as donkeys, mares, goats and sheep and they do this in preference to copulation with women.[7] There are also women who copulate with animals[8] such as dogs and donkeys.

Some cases are known where men have used ducks and geese and other kinds of fowl for their pleasures.

* * *

There are those hideous creatures of the night, the ghouls (AL GHILAN) who are actually mortal and perverted men, who will copulate with the corpses of women when they are able to find them.[9]

They will dig a woman's body up in the night, and then they will copulate with it. May Allah curse them and treat them eternally to his most severe punishments.

* * *

There are men and women who are so degenerate that they will urinate and defecate on each other[10] before they copulate, which practice they claim gives them added excitement and pleasures. Such men sometimes prefer to enter the women through their anuses.

May Allah curse them always.

* * *

There are men who are cruel and must beat and whip the women before they copulate with them.[11] They are unable to otherwise get their erection and the punishment inflicted on these unfortunate women, who are mostly their slaves, is sometimes beyond the imagination of sane men.

Strangely, there are men who like to be whipped and beaten[12] by their women before they will mount them.

* * *

There are beasts in human form who will abduct small children, both boys and girls, and who will cruelly use them for their unnatural pleasures and when they are finished they may kill them.[13]

It is sometimes discovered that these poor children had been tortured most horribly before they were killed.

Such beasts will surely come to reside forever in the hottest precipices of Hell.

* * *

There are men who will copulate with women and then unmercifully kill them, after they are through with their pleasures.

These unfortunate women are either strangled, or killed by having their throats cut or they may be despatched by being stabbed wildly and with maniacal frenzy all over their bodies.[14]

* * *

Now I shall describe the abominable practitioners of pederasty (AL LOUAAT) who, may Allah curse them, are ever on the increase. It is most disturbing that the practice of pederasty is becoming very widely spread in our society both in its higher and lower echelons, Some monarchs both in ancient times and recently have been known to be its constant and avid practitioners.

I hesitate with distaste in writing about such disgusting and blasphemous practices, but the cause of truth and science drives me to tell all that I know.

It is because of such practices that Allah finally smote and destroyed the people of the Prophet Lot (LOUT)[15] in ancient times and I am in hopes that such will be the will of Allah again.

Pederasts are of two characters. There are the active pederasts who seek other men so that they may mount them and penetrate their anuses with their penises and they will obtain their pleasures thus. It is known that the men who are mounted may also obtain their pleasures, either spontaneously, or by having their penises fondled by the hands of their active partners.

Most active pederasts prefer to acquire young, hairless and immature boys, whom they prefer to older men.[17] Thus are many innocent boys lured into these practices and many will become active pederasts when they grow to manhood.

* * *

107

The second type is the passive pederasts,[18] who submits to being mounted, and his anus penetrated by another man's penis.

It is known that these men or boys will initially feel no pleasure when they are penetrated, only pain and discomfort, but they will submit for various reasons. However, they may come to feel a kind of perverse pleasure[19] as time goes by and some may go into their orgasms soon after they are penetrated. Lubricants of various kinds are used to effect the penetration of the penis, such as grease, oil or saliva from the mouth of one of the partners, so as to overcome the resistance of the muscles of the anus. But after some time the anal muscles will become permanently relaxed and penetration will become possible and easy without the aid of lubricants. When this state is reached the men will surely develop incontinence of the bowels and they must go to stool immediately and on the slightest urge, or they may defecate in their clothes.

Such are Allah's initial punishments for all transgressors.

* * *

Other forms of abnormal contacts sometimes occur between men, where actual pederasty is not practiced.

These are men and boys who will manipulate each other's penises to the point of orgasm in each other's hands, while they may be kissing and fondling each other.

There are men and boys who will lick and suck each other's penises to the point of orgasm in each other's mouths.

May Allah curse them one and all.

* * *

Women who are closely confined together, in large hareems for instance, and who have no men to copulate with, will often form unnatural attachments to each other.

These women will lie together and will fondle each other's bodies. They will kiss each other ardently in their mouths and they will suck at each other's breasts. They will fondle and kiss and suck at each other's vulvas and clitorises and they will rub their vulvas and thighs and clitorises against each other while they are embracing. These women are the lesbians (AL MUSAHIQAAT).

At some time or another, all these women will experience clitoral orgasms and some will come to prefer these relations to the otherwise hurried and unsatisfied relations with men and many may become disgusted if approached by men.[20] Or they may enter into copulation with men against their will, but they will derive no pleasure from such unions.

THE MORBID CONDITIONS OF MEN AND WOMEN

It is not my purpose here to give a detailed account of all the morbid conditions that afflict men and women, as this is not a medical treatise. Rather, I shall give brief descriptions of some of the common conditions that affect the organs of procreation and copulation, so that the reader may become aware of their occurrence in him or in his women. He may attempt at the cures that I shall recommend, or he may seek other advice after he recognizes that such advice becomes mandatory.

Thus men and women may look forward to a healthy and pleasurable relation, which would otherwise be marred by pain and discomfort if any of these conditions were allowed to persist and proliferate without effective treatment.

THE WOMAN

Inflammation of the Vulva (ILTIHAB AL FARJ)[1]

This condition is characterised by much redness and marked swelling of the vulval lips and body. There may be considerable burning and itching and sometimes pain which may be so severe that the woman can sit or walk with much difficulty, or not at all, and thus she may be forced constantly to lie

109

on her back with her thighs wide apart. In extreme cases ulcers, which may fill with pus, will form on the lips.

The causes of this condition, which may appear very suddenly, or may be noted initially as a very mild itch of the vulva, and worsen in a few days, are thought to be because of the failure of the woman to wash and clean her vulva properly, especially after copulation.

In washing the vulva, only mild soap must be used, as the strong kind will sometimes produce a severe irritation which may lead to the inflammation of the vulva.

The treatment of this condition is to have the woman sit in a tub of hot water, in which a small amount of the oil of thyme is added. The temperature of the water must be such as not to aggravate the inflammation. More water should be added periodicallly to keep the temperature constant. The woman should sit thus for an hour each day until the inflammation disappears, and this may happen within four or five days, even in the severe conditions.

If the woman is unable to sit down, hot, wet compresses should be applied periodically to her vulva while she is lying down.

Putrefaction of the Vagina and Uterus (TA'AFUN AL MAHBAL WA AL RAHM)[2]

This is a condition which varies from the simple to the very grave. It is characterised initially by the appearance of purulent discharge from the orifice of the vagina. Later on pain in the general area may become a major symptom.

The discharge may be of a minor nature, or it may be profuse and in the mild cases it is clear and yellowish, but with a putrid odour. On contact with the vulva, this discharge may produce severe itching and the woman must constantly wash her vulva to avoid such irritation.

The causes of this condition are not known, although I suspect that they may be due to certain imbalances in the woman's physical system.

110

The minor cases which usually afflict younger women may be treated as follows: Place the woman in an upside down position against the wall, with her legs spread apart to expose her vulva. Into the vagina insert a smooth and well-lubricated funnel of appropriate size. Such funnel, which will be made of wood, must be free of slivers and its stem should be inserted for about the width of five fingers into the vagina canal. Once the funnel is in position, pour very slowly into it a warm, mild solution of vinegar (one part vinegar to five part of water) until the stem is full, then draw the funnel out of the woman, very slowly.

The woman should then remain in her inverted position for a few minutes. This treatment is best repeated every other day until the discharge stops and in uncomplicated cases this will be within two or three weeks.

In older women a thick, frothy, bloody and very foul smelling discharge may sometimes be seen and this condition will always have a very grave prognosis.[3] The woman thus afflicted will die when the putrefaction spreads to her uterus and rots it away. Such women will die in great pain within one or two years. There is no hope for them, and may Allah hasten their end, so that they may not unduly suffer.

May Allah forgive me, for in such cases I recommend that wine and other spirits be given to these women[4], so that their pains may be dulled in their last agonizing days.

Painful Copulation (AWJA'A AL JIMA'A)[5]

Pain during copulation may be primary when the virgin is deflowered and the pain may continue to occur with each successive act, even though the hymen may have healed.

The other kind of pain can appear at any time during the woman's life and after she has been enjoying copulation.

I suspect that the majority of the first kind is because the women became so frightened as a result of being abused and hurt on their first night. Subsequently all their muscles would cramp painfully[6] when they are entered. There may be other causes, such as the possession of unusually small vaginas, thus making all entries painful, or there may be unseen lesions or irregularities inside the canal, which will cause pain when rubbed by the penetrating penis.

In the first group, treatment must be directed to the men, who must be taught to get their women thoroughly aroused before they are entered. Thus, when they are penetrated, all their muscles will be in a relaxed condition and they will come to enjoy copulation and look forward to it.

When the woman complains of pain during copulation, the man must stop all attempts at mounting her again until the cause of the pain is found and treated. If the condition is found to be intractable, the man must seek his pleasure elsewhere.

Tumors of the Breast (TADARUN AL THADI)

The breast of the woman may be afflicted with growths which usually occur on the outer side in one breast or the other, but very rarely in both. These start as small round lumps which can be felt to move rather freely under the skin. Some will remain small and are of no consequence. However, among older women, these growths may enlarge rapidly until they break the skin and huge abscesses will form on the breast and they cannot be cured.[7]

The only thing that can be done to help alleviate the suffering of these women is constantly to apply cold, wet compresses to these areas, so that the oozing pus may be absorbed and will not contaminate the skin around the breast. Pain will ultimately become very severe and will spread from the breast to many other parts of the body,[8] and the woman will die in a short time.

Here, I also recommend without reservation that these women should be given wines and spirits constantly to dull their otherwise unbearable pains and suffering.

112

Impotence (AL U'NNAH)

This is the most unpopular condition that afflicts the man, and with great reason, for he who is thus affected will cease to be the practitioner of the supreme pleasures of this life. He will become an outcast from his women and will be transformed into an object of pity and perhaps derision and contempt.

The man, through the ages, has been very concerned about this condition, more than any other, and thousands of recipes and cures have been tried or proposed to slow his inevitable encounter with impotence.

Impotence is of two varieties. The first is the state which results from senility and old age. Here it is a permanent condition and nothing can be done to cure it. The man thus afflicted may at various times, due to the ingestion of certain potions and drugs, cause his penis to become erect for very short periods. But he can derive no real pleasure or satisfaction, because he will experience no orgasm and, what is more important, he can give the woman no pleasure from such a brief encounter.

The man's body, in old age, shrivels and becomes repulsive to the young and healthy women. Thus exposing an erect penis which is coupled to a shaky, wizened and dried up body, must only add to her distaste and revulsion.

It is wise for the old man who has reached this state to forsake all attempts at copulation. His final hours are much better spent in preparing himself for the inevitable journey to the Hereafter.

With the loss of the pleasures of the flesh, more time may be spent in the pursuit of the pleasures of the mind and the spirit, which in old age are as thrilling as the pleasures of the flesh were in the younger days.

* * *

Many cases of impotence occur in the young and middle aged, and here the attempt at the earliest cure of these cases is justified, for these, when cured, will still have many years left in which they may enjoy copulation. Fortunately, in most cases the periods of impotence are brief and the cures are simple.

Some events in the life of the man will cause impotence. The most common is when the man becomes affected by a weakening and debilitating disease. In this case, the man's whole physical system is weakened, including all his muscles and organs and he will become impotent, which condition may remain for some time after the cure of the disease has been effected. Here, therapy is directed at putting strength back into the man and once this happens, his impotence will be replaced with new abilities and desires.

Strength and vigour will return quickly by eating heartily again, and the best foods are the meats of every variety and in great quantities. Of special benefit will be the consumption of the testicles of sheep, goats, cattle and camels and of medicinal value are the penises and testicles of crocodiles[9] (which come dried and powdered) and these are potent and invigorating to the man, and he will soon feel his powers returning. The eating of raw eggs, if they are fresh, is very beneficial. Small portions of ambergris[10] (ANBAR) has been tried with very good results.

There are a myriad other potions which are used. However, their effect may produce only temporary erection and the man can surely not copulate effectively if his muscles are too weak to hold him or make him move.

* * *

Some men have the understandable difficulty in maintaining their erections with women whom, although they may still love, such as older and loyal wives, no longer excite them.

114

This condition is embarrassing to both the man and the woman, especially to the man who may want sincerely to mount the woman to please her, but who cannot rouse himself, or finds that his erection soon fades away after he has entered her.

There is no morbidity in these cases, and I can only advise these men to close their eyes and imagine they are copulating with beautiful and exciting women.

Allah will help these men to maintain their erection, for they will be doing works of great charity.

Perpetual Erection (AL INTISAB AL DA'EM)[11]

Although the state of perpetual erection of the penis is the wish and dream of many foolish men, it sometimes afflicts a few unfortunate men. This is no pleasurable phenomenon, but a highly morbid condition. The penis will swell and appear as in erection but it will be very tender and painful to the touch. Needless to say, copulation is impossible.

The swelling and erection may be quite persistent and leeches (AL ALAQ) may have to be attached to the penis to draw the excess blood out of it and this may cause the swelling to subside. Even then, and very often, the penis will swell painfully again when the leeches are removed.

The penis should be surrounded with soft padding for its protection from injury and care should be taken to elevate the bed sheets away from it.

Sometimes forcible massage may help to drive the excess blood out of the penis, but this is a very painful and drastic procedure, which should be resorted to when all other treatment fails. The man must be held down by others while this treatment is being carried out.

Wrapping cold compresses around the penis may sometimes help to shrink it.

Inflammation of the Head of the Penis (ILTIHAB RA'AS AL QADHEEB)

This condition may result from copulating with a woman who is suffering from the putrefaction of the vagina. Active pederasts are also plagued with this condition and this is understandable in view of the nature of their vile practices.

The head of the penis becomes swollen and very red in color, and it will burn to the touch. Urination may become difficulty and painful if the orifice of the penis is swollen shut.

To treat a penis thus afflicted, dip it many times a day in a very strong and warm tea solution.

Putrefaction of the Urinary Canal (TA'AFUN QANAT AL QADHEEB)[12]

This often times is a very serious condition which is perhaps caused by the absorption into the canal of the penis of some harmful ingredients from the woman during copulation, if the woman is suffering from the putrefaction of the vagina.

Extreme pain and a burning sensation when urinating are the two usual symptoms, together with the discharging of purulent material resembling pus and which smells very badly. The pain may spread to the testicles and upper thighs and to the belly and back.

Sometimes the canal will become completely blocked and the man will not be able to urinate. Here a long, blunt needle should be inserted as far as it will go, in an effort to open the canal. If this attempt fails, the man will collapse and die in a few days.

Usually, such a condition, if there are no complications, is self limiting and will clear up within a few weeks without treatment.

116

Growths in the Scrotum (TADARUN AL SAFN)

Lumps can sometimes grow in the scrotum and they may be painful or not, and they may grow to huge sizes and the man will die soon afterwards.[13] In the meantime he will become impotent.

There is no cure for such cases.[14]

NOTES

CHAPTER III

1. FEE AL SHOUDHOUDH WA AL HALAT AL MARADIYYAH FEE AL RIJAL WA AL NISA'A
2. Hermaphroditism is defined as the modification in the primary sex characteristics (the general organs), towards the structure that is typical in the genitals of the opposite sex.
3. Male androgyny.
4. Female androgyny.
5. The male transvestite.
6. The female transvestite.
7. Male bestiality. According to Kinsey, in certain Western areas of the U.S.A., as high as 65 per cent of the boys and men have had sexual contact of one kind or another with animals.
8. Female bestiality.
9. This practice is termed necrophilia and two forms have been differentiated, one which follows immediately upon sexual murder, in which case the murderer copulates with the freshly killed corpse of his victim, or the necrophile obtains a corpse by digging it up from its grave, as described by the author.
10. Urolagnia and coprolagnia. Extreme cases of these aberrations are when the men or the women actually consume the urine or excreta of their partners.
11. These are cases of actual physical and sexual sadism.
12. Physical and sexual masochism.
13. Sadism against children may begin with the relatively harmless psychological sadism where the child will not be actually harmed, but perhaps manhandled. But this may develop into serious sadistic abuse and later to physical injury and murder..
14. The author is describing sexual murder and perhaps one of the forms of necrophilia.

15. Lot is a character of ancient times, associated with Hebrew history. He was the grandson of Terah and the nephew of Abraham, with whom he left Haran in North Mesopotamia, proceeded to Canaan, journeyed into Egypt, returned and afterwards separated from Abraham, with Lot choosing a settlement near Sodom (location is uncertain, but thought to be north of the Dead Sea or now covered by the Dead Sea). Lot was supposed to have been forewarned of the imminent destruction of Sodom because of the immorality of its people and their perverted sexual practices. He escaped with his family; however, his wife was turned into a pillar of salt as the penalty for looking back on the city. Lot is considered as a prophet by Islam. The term sodomy is derived from the name of the city.

16. No great stigma is attached to the active pederast by the Arabs.

17. The urge towards active pederasty among the Arabs, in certain countries and communities, may largely be due to the absence of opportunities for heterosexual contacts. This may explain the attraction that most active pederasts have towards young, hairless boys whose smooth skin and soft bodies remind them of women and thus excite them.

18. The passive pederast is held by the Arabs to derision and utter contempt.

19. Perhaps because of masochism or physically due to the stimulation of their prostate gland. It is also known that the membrane of the anus and rectum of some men is very sensitive and they may derive pleasure from its stimulation by the partner's penis.

20. These are the true lesbians.

THE WOMAN

1. This condition is termed vulvitis and it is defined as an inflammatory reaction affecting the vulva, from many diverse causes. The application of cream and ointment containing antibiotics and cortisone derivitives is recommended, plus systematic antibiotic treatment when the condition is serious or chronic.

2. This condition is termed leukorrhea and it is defined as a gynecological disorder which is characterised by abnormal discharges from the female genital tract. Infection by bacteria, protozoa or fungus is the direct cause and it is treated by systematic administration of the appropriate antibiotic, and by the insertion of medicated suppositories.

3. The author may be describing some of the symptoms of malignancy (cancer) of the female genital organs.

4. The consumption of alcoholic beverages is strictly forbidden by Islam and under all circumstances.

5. This condition is known as dyspareunia.

6. The painful cramping of the vaginal muscles during coitus is termed as vaginismus.

7. The author is perhaps describing cancer of the breast and the only cure available now is to amputate the affected breast (mastectomy).

8. The phenomenon of the spreading of the cancer from one organ to the other (metastasis) is described.

THE MAN

9. It cannot be ascertained what invigorating ingredients are contained in such a potion.

10. Ambergris is a fatty substance found often floating in tropical seas or cast on the beaches of tropical islands. It occurs in lumps from half an ounce to a hundred pounds in weight, and it is a secretion that is formed in the stomach and intestinal tract of the sperm whale. Ambergris is composed of about 80% cholesterol plus fatty oil, aberin and benzoic acid. It has chiefly been used in the perfumery industry as tincture and essence for fixing delicate perfumes, but now it is largely supplanted by synthetic chemicals. The Arabs and many other peoples of Asia believe it to have great aphrodisiac properties, but this is not substantial by scientific experimental evidence.

11. This very painful condition is called priapism. It is known to result from either neurological diseases or painful stimuli such as bladder calculs (stones), urethritis (infection of the urethra) or prostitis (infection of the prostate gland), or from obstruction of the blood vessels that drain the penis. The cure is effected by the removal of the cause.

12. The author is perhaps describing gonorrhea and urethritis.

13. This is a description of malignant (cancerous) growths in the scrotum.

14. Cancer of the testicles and scrotum can be cured either by an orchiectomy (castration) or radiation, or both.

119

CHAPTER IV

OF MEN AND WOMEN[1]

"Men are in charge of women because Allah has made the
one of them to excel the other and because they spend their
property. So good women are the obedient ones"
                              THE HOLY QUR'AN

KNOW YE that I have almost reached the
end of my treatise. What is left are the random thoughts that
I shall now put down regarding the different natures of men
and women.

Allah has decreed that men must be made responsible for
women. Thus He absolved women of independent struggle
and achievement.

Women's minds are less adept than men's, and men must
protect women and provide for them, and thus women have
no need for strength. All they need for adequate survival is
their personal charm and allure so that men may want to
keep them as theirs and they will die in their defense and
the defense of their children.

Such is the destiny of men.

*   *   *

The woman is endowed by Allah with a great and persistent urge to procreate; more so than the man. Thus she
looks for fulfillment and for protection to the virile and
strong man.

The woman is irresistibly attracted to the man of strength
and courage and virility, for in his embrace she will find
her haven of physical gratification and security.

The woman has no need, neither does she have compassion for the weak man and she will look on such a man with loathing and contempt, because in his weakness she sees a reflection of her own weakness.

If her lot falls with the weak man, she becomes greatly disturbed, since this would mean insecurity and possible danger for her and her children. She cannot gain solace from him, in body or in spirit. She will become cold and unresponsive and she may lash out at him in all devious manners, so that she may punish him for his weakness which is causing her unhappiness.

* * *

The fulfilled woman is an exquisitely sweet creature. She is a delight to the eyes and to the body and spirit of the man and through her he will have a glimpse of Paradise.

* * *

The unfulfilled woman is a terrible creature, for in her lack of fulfillment she has lost everything and her life has become as barren as the great Sahara and her spirit has become as dark as eternal night. The Devil and all his mischief dwells in her soul.

* * *

The Man's ultimate weapon is his mind, the woman's ultimate weapon is her body.

* * *

Allah has said of women: "AND THEIR CUNNING IS GREAT." There is great wisdom and meaning here. Women are cunning because they are weak and dependent, as cunningness is basically a trait of the weak. It is also a trait of the weak man.

If the woman is protected and loved as she should be, she will not need to be cunning, but she will be as sweet as a child.

Women are like children; they are what you make them. Spoil them and you shall reap misery. Mistreat them and you

121

shall reap Allah's wrath. Given them your love and attention and they will bloom like beautitful flowers.

* * *

Women are primarily creatures of sensual pleasures. To them nothing else matters. Satisfy their tastes and gratify their bodies and they will close their eyes to your every transgression and they will become your slaves, willingly and gladly.

* * *

When a woman desires one man and refuses all other men, she is said to be in love with that man. She can derive no pleasure from other men.

* * *

When a man is in love with a woman, he will derive his greatest pleasure from her, but he can derive much pleasure from other women.

* * *

There are men who will love certain women desperately and to the exclusion of all other women and they will remain faithful to them. Such is not normal and these men are lacking in their masculinity.

* * *

The woman likes to be always with the man she loves and to share all her time with him, under all circumstances and conditions.

* * *

When a man loves to be constantly with the woman he loves, to the exclusion of all activities without her or away from her, he is lacking in his masculinity.

To please a man, compliment his mind. To please a woman, compliment her beauty and charms.

* * *

Marriage is everything to a woman. It is her whole life and occupation. Marriage is only an episode in a man's life.

The woman's existence in society outside of marriage cannot be justified. It will be like a useless tree that bears no fruit.

Man's existence in society is justified only by his intellectual achievements.

* * *

Do not fight among you because of women, for thus you will become like the animals.

A woman who purposely spreads discord among men by using her body as bait is evil, and she must be isolated from the company of men. Such women usually will derive great sexual excitement from seeing men fight over them and their thrill will increase if blood is spilled.

* * *

Show great compassion towards the adulteress, for most probably you have driven her into that road by your callousness. However, you cannot forgive her and return her to your bed, but you must deliver her back to her people, or you must sell her, if she is your slave.

* * *

Do not copulate with the woman who has lost her wits, for she will not truly understand what you are doing to her, although her vagina may become moist. But copulating with her will be like the mounting of a dumb animal.

Sometimes it will happen that the vagina of such a woman will clasp the man's penis like a bitch will clasp the male dog. In such cases, the woman must be made to lose consciousness by hitting her on the head with a blunt and padded stick, as only thus will her vagina relax its grip.[2]

* * *

Do not copulate with the woman who is an idiot, for all your children will turn out like her.

* * *

Do not copulate with the woman who has reached her menopause, for she has become like a gnarled vine that bears

123

no fruit. Her vagina will be dry and irritating, her breasts will be sagging and wrinkled and the taste of her saliva will be stale.

*   *   *

The sweetest woman can be turned into a shrew by the man if he excites her but does not fulfill her. To tame her and bring her back into sweetness, he must copulate with her and bring forth her pleasures and she will change immediately, as night changes into day.

*   *   *

Never punish a woman who disobeys you by withholding yourself away from her in copulation,[3] if she still indicates that she desires you. It is more merciful to spank her. Beware, however, because some women derive intense and voluptuous pleasures when they are spanked, and the object of the punishment is defeated.

In spanking a woman, never hit her on the breast or on the belly. It is best to place her over your knee and to spank her soundly on her buttocks.

Like children, although the actual spanking will cause pain, the women will appreciate it because it will mean that you cared enough about them to have taken the time for their discipline.

Later it is very wise to copulate with them, to show that all is well and it is best to show extra tenderness and skill, and your reward will be great in their passionate response, because they too will have it in their minds to please you more than usual.

*   *   *

Know ye that I have finally and by the grace of Allah reached to the end of my treatise, which may be my last work. And I thank Allah for His help.

I have but one more remark and that is to remind you, lest you have forgotten, that Allah's purpose in bestowing on you the pleasurable gift of copulation is to procreate. To insure this, you must copulate daily between the woman's

124

menstrual periods. Only thus can you ensure that she will become pregnant, as Allah only knows her exact date of readiness for copulation.[4]

So be of good heart and vigour, if you want to increase your progeny, and enter the woman and deposit your seed in her daily, until she shows signs that she has become pregnant. Only then can you get respite from your pleasant labours and may you, with the blessing of Allah, always live in happiness among your frolicsome women and children.

* * *

NOTES

1. FEE AL RIJAL WA AL NISA'A
2. The method of resolving this embarrassing problem is to allow the woman to be anaesthetised by a physician. Her muscles will thus relax and the grip on the man's penis will be eased, allowing him to withdraw it. But if no medical help is available or wanted for reasons of modesty, have the woman breath into a small paper or plastic bag until she passes out and this will result in the instant relaxation of her muscles. This is not a dangerous procedure, and the woman will revive without ill effect when the bag is removed from her mouth.
3. This is contrary to the teachings of Islam, which prescribes thus, in accordance with the works of the Holy Qur'an: ". . . AS FOR THOSE WOMEN FROM WHOM YOU FEAR REBELLION, ADMONISH THEM AND BANISH THEM TO BEDS APART AND SCOURGE THEM. THEN IF THEY OBEY YOU, SEEK NOT A WAY AGAINST THEM . . . . . ."
4. The periods of ovulation of the woman were not known to the author and this accounts for his advice. It is now known that ovulation occurs during the middle of the cycle (halfway between two consecutive menstrual periods). In cycles that are of 28 days duration, ovulation takes place from 12 to 16 days before the beginning of the next menstrual period.